GENERAL EDITOR: CHRISTOPHER RICKS

THOMAS HARDY:
SELECTED POEMS

THOMAS HARDY was born at Higher Bockhampton, near
Dorchester, on 2 June 1840. He was educated locally at the village
school, and later in Dorchester. At sixteen he was articled to the
Dorchester architect and church restorer John Hicks, although he
continued his studies under the guidance of Horace Moule, a
Cambridge graduate, whose later suicide affected Hardy and his
writing deeply. In 1862 he went to London to pursue his architectural
career and also began writing at this time. He returned to Dorset in
1867 to become assistant to John Hicks, at the same time beginning
his first novel, *The Poor Man and the Lady*, of which only fragments
remain. In 1870 Hardy was sent to St Juliot in Cornwall, and it was
here that he met his first wife, Emma Gifford, whom he married in
1874; in the same year *Far from the Madding Crowd* was published
and met with considerable success. In the previous three years he had
published *Desperate Remedies* (1871), *Under the Greenwood Tree*
(1872) and *A Pair of Blue Eyes* (1873). In 1878 Hardy moved back to
London, and in this year *The Return of the Native* appeared. His
reputation as a writer grew and he be[...]
London's literary circles. In 1885 he [...]
Max Gate, and over the next three yea[...]
Casterbridge (1886), which many regar[...]
The Woodlanders (1887) and his firs[...]
Wessex Tales (1888). In 1891 *Tess of the [...]*
in 1895 his last novel, *Jude the Obscure*. During the latter part of his
life Hardy devoted himself to poetry, publishing his first collection of
verse, *Wessex Poems*, in 1898. He also worked on his autobiography,
The Early Life of Thomas Hardy (published posthumously in 1928),
at the same time burning his old letters, notebooks and private
papers. Thomas Hardy died on 11 January 1928.

HARRY THOMAS has edited *The Hopwood Anthology: Five Decades of
American Poetry* and *Berryman's Understanding: Reflections on the
Poetry of John Berryman*. His translation of Joseph Brodsky's major
work, *Gorbunov and Gorchakov*, appeared in *To Urania* (Penguin
1988). [...] He teaches at
Davids[...]

Thomas Hardy
Selected Poems

Edited with a Preface by
HARRY THOMAS

PENGUIN BOOKS

For Lee Gerlach

PENGUIN BOOKS

Published by the Penguin Group
Penguin Books Ltd, 27 Wrights Lane, London W8 5TZ, England
Penguin Books USA Inc., 375 Hudson Street, New York, New York 10014, USA
Penguin Books Australia Ltd, Ringwood, Victoria, Australia
Penguin Books Canada Ltd, 10 Alcorn Avenue, Toronto, Ontario, Canada M4V 3B2
Penguin Books (NZ) Ltd, 182–190 Wairau Road, Auckland 10, New Zealand

Penguin Books Ltd, Registered Offices: Harmondsworth, Middlesex, England

First published 1993
3 5 7 9 10 8 6 4 2

Selection, Preface and Notes copyright © Harry Thomas, 1993
All rights reserved

The moral right of the editor has been asserted

10/11.5 pt Monotype Ehrhardt
Typeset by Datix International Limited, Bungay, Suffolk
Printed in England by Clays Ltd, St Ives plc

Contents

Preface

Thomas Hardy worked as an architect's assistant until the age of thirty-two, and spent the better part of three decades writing fifteen novels and three volumes of short stories, but he was first and last a poet. 'Domicilium', the earliest of the poems that he preserved, dates from 1857, when Hardy was seventeen. During his years in London, the 1860s, he devoted what time he could spare from his architectural labours to reading Dryden's *Aeneid*, Shakespeare's sonnets, *Paradise Lost*, and the poetry of Tennyson, Browning, Palgraves's *Golden Treasury*, and – his deepest passion after its publication in 1866 – Swinburne's *Poems and Ballads*. Naturally, without meaning to, he memorized for life much of what he read. Also during these years he was writing sonnets, ballads, and innovative poems combining complex song-like stanzas and ordinary speech rhythms. One day in 1866 he wrote 'Neutral Tones'. When, in March of 1870, he travelled to St Juliot to make drawings for the restoration of the church there, the young woman who greeted him at the rectory door, and who would later become his first wife, noticed 'a blue paper sticking out of his pocket'. Forty years later she recalled that to her surprise the paper had 'proved to be the MS of a poem, and not a plan of the church'.

By 1895 Hardy the novelist was wealthy enough to go back to being Hardy the poet. In the preface to his first book of poetry, *Wessex Poems and Other Verses* (1898), he revealed that he had continued to write poems during the decades of the fiction, but noted sadly: 'In some few cases the verses were turned into prose and printed as such, it having been unanticipated at that time that they might see the light'. Before his death in 1928 Hardy brought more than nine hundred poems to light, as well as the three-volume epic in verse, *The Dynasts*, and the verse play, *The Famous Tragedy of the Queen of Cornwall*.

William Empson remarked more than fifty years ago that 'a

working selection from Hardy's mass of bad poetry is much needed'. No two readers will agree on the size of that 'mass' (Philip Larkin, one of Hardy's keenest readers, protested famously that he 'would not wish Hardy's *Collected Poems* a single page shorter'), but many readers since Empson have reasserted the need for 'a working selection', and perhaps most have felt it. Though the editors of some previous selections have sought to satisfy it, I believe that the need still exists. It has not been my intention in making this selection to represent the range – chronological, thematic or formal – of Hardy's poetry, but to present the best poems. In an effort to keep from imposing too objectionably personal an idea of 'best' on the volume, I have tried to stay open to the enthusiasm of other readers for poems which I might have thought to exclude.

To Joseph Brodsky, Lee Gerlach, Donald Hall, and Christopher Ricks, I express my gratitude.

Table of Dates

1840   2 June: Born at Higher Bockhampton, the first child of Thomas Hardy, a mason, and Jemima (née Hand), formerly a servant.

1842–4   Learns to read before he is three; begins to play the fiddle.

1848   Attends Mrs Julia Augusta Martin's school at Lower Bockhampton. His mother gives him the *Aeneid* (Dryden's translation), *Rasselas* and *Paul and Virginia*.

1850–53   Attends Isaac Last's British School in Dorchester, a Nonconformist institution established by the British and Foreign Bible Society.

1853–6   Attends Isaac Last's new Congregationalist 'Academy' where he begins to study Latin. Teaches in Stinsford Sunday School.

1856   Apprenticed to John Hicks, a Dorchester architect; meets William Barnes, poet and philologist, whose school is next door.

1857   Meets and comes under the intellectual influence of Horace Moule (born 1832), fourth son of the Reverend Henry Moule, vicar of Fordington, and formerly a classical scholar at Queens' College, Cambridge. Begins to write poetry.

1860   Reads and discusses with Horace Moule *Essays and Reviews* and *The Origin of Species*. Until 1865, considers a career in the Church.

1862   Moves to London where, in May, he begins his career as an architect in the office of Arthur Blomfield. Spends his lunch-hour daily at the National Gallery.

1865   'How I Built Myself a House' appears in *Chambers's Journal* – his first publication.

1866   Writes and sends poems to editors of London magazines, who send them back.

1867   Ill, returns to Higher Bockhampton. Begins seeing
        Tryphena Sparks (born 1851), daughter of his mother's
        older sister.
        Autumn: Begins first draft of *The Poor Man and the
        Lady*, a novel Macmillan rejects in August 1868.

1869   March: George Meredith, serving as a publisher's
        reader, advises him against publication of *The Poor Man
        and the Lady*.
        Summer: Moves to Weymouth to work for G. R. Crick-
        may, architect; buys a ring for Tryphena Sparks, who is
        teaching at nearby Coryates; writes several poems.
        September: Starts a new novel, *Desperate Remedies*.

1870   7 March: In St Juliot, Cornwall, on architectural busi-
        ness, meets Emma Lavinia Gifford, his future wife.
        May: His second novel, *Desperate Remedies*, accepted
        for publication; moves to London to pursue his career
        in architecture.
        August: Visits Emma in Cornwall.

1871   March: Publication of *Desperate Remedies*; moves back
        to Weymouth to work for Crickmay.
        May: Spends several weeks at St Juliot.
        Summer: Begins writing *Under the Greenwood Tree*.
        October: Visits Emma, who encourages him to devote
        himself entirely to writing.

1872   Works as an architect in London.
        June: Publication of *Under the Greenwood Tree*.
        September: His fourth novel, *A Pair of Blue Eyes*, for
        which he receives a £200 advance, begins to run serially
        in *Tinsley's Magazine*.
        December: Leslie Stephen offers to publish anything he
        writes in the *Cornhill Magazine*.

1873   May: Publication of *A Pair of Blue Eyes*.
        June–July: Breaks off with Tryphena Sparks; becomes
        engaged to Emma.
        September: Horace Moule commits suicide in Cam-
        bridge.
        Autumn: Begins *Far from the Madding Crowd* (1874).

1874   17 September: Marries Emma at St Peter's Church,
        London; honeymoon in Brighton, Rouen and Paris.

Autumn: Lives in Surbiton, Surrey, near London.

1875   Moves to Westbourne Grove, London; begins writing *The Hand of Ethelberta* (1876).

1876–8   'Idyll' at Sturminster Newton. Composition, then publication of *The Return of the Native* (1878). Figures in London literary scene.

1880–81   October: Publication of *The Trumpet-Major*.
October–April: Bedridden, dictates *A Laodicean* (1881) to Emma.

1882   October: Publication of *Two on a Tower*.

1883   June: Moves to Dorchester.

1885   29 June: Moves into house he calls Max Gate, one mile south-east of Dorchester, where, save for summers in London, he lives until his death.

1886   May: Publication of *The Mayor of Casterbridge*.
Summer: Does research in the British Museum for *The Dynasts* (1904, 1906, 1908).
7 October: William Barnes dies.

1887   March: Publication of *The Woodlanders*.
March–April: Tours Italy with Emma.

1888   May: Publication of *Wessex Tales*, a volume of short stories.

1890   17 March: Tryphena Sparks dies.

1891   May: Publication of *A Group of Noble Dames* (stories).
November: Publication of *Tess of the D'Urbervilles*.

1892   20 July: His father dies.
October–December: Serial publication of *The Well-Beloved* (1897).

1893   19 May: In Dublin, meets and becomes infatuated with Mrs Florence Henniker.

1894   February: Publication of *Life's Little Ironies* (stories).

1895   November: Publication of *Jude the Obscure*; furore ensues; his marriage sours.

1896   September: Walks the battlefield at Waterloo.
October: Notes in his journal 'the end of prose'; returns to writing poetry.

1897   27 June: In Lausanne, Switzerland, observes the 110th anniversary of Gibbon's completion there of *The Decline and Fall of the Roman Empire*.

1922   May: Publication of *Late Lyrics and Earlier*.
1923   July: Is host to the Prince of Wales at Max Gate.
        November: Publication of *The Famous Tragedy of the
        Queen of Cornwall*, a play in verse.
1925   November: Publication of *Human Shows, Far Phantasies,
        Songs and Trifles*.
1928   11 January: Dies at the age of eighty-seven. His heart
        buried in Stinsford churchyard, his ashes in Westminster
        Abbey.
        October: Publication of *Winter Words in Various Moods
        and Metres*.

Further Reading

Editions

The Complete Poems of Thomas Hardy, ed. James Gibson, Macmillan, 1976.

The Dynasts, 3 vols, Macmillan, 1920.

The Complete Poetical Works of Thomas Hardy, ed. Samuel Hynes, 3 vols, Oxford: Clarendon Press, 1982–5.

Thomas Hardy's Personal Writings, ed. Harold Orel, University of Kansas Press, 1966.

Letters

The Collected Letters of Thomas Hardy, ed. Richard Little Purdy and Michael Millgate, 7 vols, Oxford: Clarendon Press, 1978–88.

Biography

Evelyn Hardy and Robert Gittings, eds., *Some Recollections by Emma Hardy*, Oxford University Press, 1961. Includes valuable notes on Hardy's use of these 'recollections' in several poems.

Florence Emily Hardy, *The Life of Thomas Hardy, 1840–1928*, Macmillan, 1965. The one-volume edition of *The Early Life of Thomas Hardy, 1840–1891* (1928) and *The Later Years of Thomas Hardy, 1892–1928* (1930). A ruse: Hardy himself wrote all but the end. (In 1985 the University of Georgia Press issued a new one-volume text edited 'on new principles' by Michael Millgate.)

Robert Gittings, *Young Thomas Hardy*, Little, Brown, 1975.

Robert Gittings, *The Older Hardy*, Little, Brown, 1978.
Michael Millgate, *Thomas Hardy: A Biography*, Random House, 1982.

Criticism and Scholarship

J. O. Bailey, *The Poetry of Thomas Hardy*, University of North Carolina Press, 1970.

R. P. Blackmur, 'The Shorter Poems of Thomas Hardy', in *The Expense of Greatness*, Peter Smith, 1940, pp. 37–73.

Joseph Brodsky, 'The poet, the loved one and the Muse', *Times Literary Supplement*, 26 October–1 November 1990, pp. 1150, 1160.

Donald Davie, ed., *Agenda: Thomas Hardy Special Issue*, 10, 1972. Several essays and poems, including Davie's 'Hardy's Virgilian Purples', pp. 138–56.

Donald Davie, *Thomas Hardy and British Poetry*, Oxford University Press, 1972.

Lois Deacon and Terry Coleman, *Providence and Mr Hardy*, Hutchinson, 1966.

Thom Gunn, 'Hardy and the Ballads', in *The Occasions of Poetry*, ed. Clive Wilmer, Faber and Faber, 1982, pp. 77–105. First published in *Agenda*, 10, 1972.

Samuel Hynes, *The Pattern of Hardy's Poetry*, University of North Carolina Press, 1961.

Philip Larkin, 'Wanted: Good Hardy Critic', in *Required Writing*, Faber and Faber, 1983, pp. 168–74.

F. R. Leavis, 'Reality and Sincerity', *Scrutiny*, Winter 1952–3, pp. 87–98.

John Middleton Murry, 'The Poetry of Mr Hardy', in *Aspects of Literature*, W. Collins Sons, 1920, pp. 121–38.

Tom Paulin, *Thomas Hardy: The Poetry of Perception*, Rowman and Littlefield, 1975.

Ezra Pound, Appendix I, in *Confucius to Cummings*, New Directions, 1964, pp. 325–9.

John Crowe Ransom, ed., *Selected Poems of Thomas Hardy*, Macmillan, 1960. Includes an introduction.

John Crowe Ransom, 'Old Age of an Eagle', in *Poems and Essays*, Alfred A. Knopf, 1955, pp. 79–87. Originally appeared in *New Republic*, 12 May 1952, pp. 16, 30–31.

William R. Rutland, *Thomas Hardy: A Study of His Writings and Their Background*, Basil Blackwell, 1938.

Delmore Schwartz, 'Poetry and Belief in Thomas Hardy', *Southern Review*, 1, 1940, pp. 64–77.

Lytton Strachey, 'Mr Hardy's New Poems', *New Statesman*, 19 December 1914.

Allen Tate, 'Hardy's Philosophic Metaphors', *Southern Review*, 1, 1940, pp. 99–108.

Raymond Williams, 'Wessex and the Border', in *The Country and the City*, Oxford University Press, 1973, pp. 197–214.

Domicilium

It faces west, and round the back and sides
High beeches, bending, hang a veil of boughs,
And sweep against the roof. Wild honeysucks
Climb on the walls, and seem to sprout a wish
(If we may fancy wish of trees and plants)
To overtop the apple-trees hard by.

Red roses, lilacs, variegated box
Are there in plenty, and such hardy flowers
As flourish best untrained. Adjoining these
Are herbs and esculents; and farther still   10
A field; then cottages with trees, and last
The distant hills and sky.

Behind, the scene is wilder. Heath and furze
Are everything that seems to grow and thrive
Upon the uneven ground. A stunted thorn
Stands here and there, indeed; and from a pit
An oak uprises, springing from a seed
Dropped by some bird a hundred years ago.

                                  In days bygone –
Long gone – my father's mother, who is now   20
Blest with the blest, would take me out to walk.
At such a time I once inquired of her
How looked the spot when first she settled here.
The answer I remember. 'Fifty years
Have passed since then, my child, and change has marked
The face of all things. Yonder garden-plots
And orchards were uncultivated slopes
O'ergrown with bramble bushes, furze and thorn:

That road a narrow path shut in by ferns,
Which, almost trees, obscured the passer-by.   30

'Our house stood quite alone, and those tall firs
And beeches were not planted. Snakes and efts
Swarmed in the summer days, and nightly bats
Would fly about our bedrooms. Heathcroppers
Lived on the hills, and were our only friends;
So wild it was when first we settled here.'

From *Wessex Poems and Other Verses* (1898)

Neutral Tones

We stood by a pond that winter day,
And the sun was white, as though chidden of God,
And a few leaves lay on the starving sod;
   – They had fallen from an ash, and were gray.

Your eyes on me were as eyes that rove
Over tedious riddles of years ago;
And some words played between us to and fro
   On which lost the more by our love.

The smile on your mouth was the deadest thing
Alive enough to have strength to die;
And a grin of bitterness swept thereby
   Like an ominous bird a-wing . . .

Since then, keen lessons that love deceives,
And wrings with wrong, have shaped to me
Your face, and the God-curst sun, and a tree,
   And a pond edged with grayish leaves.

1867

Friends Beyond

William Dewy, Tranter Reuben, Farmer Ledlow late at
     plough,
     Robert's kin, and John's, and Ned's,
And the Squire, and Lady Susan, lie in Mellstock
     churchyard now!

'Gone', I call them, gone for good, that group of local
                hearts and heads;
            Yet at mothy curfew-tide,
And at midnight when the noon-heat breathes it back from
                walls and leads,

They've a way of whispering to me – fellow-wight who yet
                abide –
            In the muted, measured note
Of a ripple under archways, or a lone cave's stillicide:

10   'We have triumphed: this achievement turns the bane to
                antidote,
            Unsuccesses to success,
Many thought-worn eves and morrows to a morrow free of
                thought.

'No more need we corn and clothing, feel of old terrestrial
                stress;
            Chill detraction stirs no sigh;
Fear of death has even bygone us: death gave all that we
                possess.'

W. D. – 'Ye mid burn the old bass-viol that I set such
                value by.'
Squire. – 'You may hold the manse in fee,
    You may wed my spouse, may let my children's
                memory of me die.'

Lady S. – 'You may have my rich brocades, my laces; take
                each household key;
20   Ransack coffer, desk, bureau;
    Quiz the few poor treasures hid there, con the
                letters kept by me.'

Far. – 'Ye mid zell my favourite heifer, ye mid let the
                charlock grow,
            Foul the grinterns, give up thrift.'
Far. Wife. – 'If ye break my best blue china, children, I
                shan't care or ho.'

All. – 'We've no wish to hear the tidings, how the people's
                fortunes shift;
            What your daily doings are;
        Who are wedded, born, divided; if your lives
                beat slow or swift.

'Curious not the least are we if our intents you make or
                mar,
            If you quire to our old tune,
    If the City stage still passes, if the weirs still roar afar.'   30

– Thus, with very gods' composure, freed those crosses late
                and soon
            Which, in life, the Trine allow
    (Why, none witteth), and ignoring all that haps beneath the
                moon,

William Dewy, Tranter Reuben, Farmer Ledlow late at
                plough,
            Robert's kin, and John's, and Ned's,
    And the Squire, and Lady Susan, murmur mildly to me
                now.

Thoughts of Phena

AT NEWS OF HER DEATH

Not a line of her writing have I,
    Not a thread of her hair,
No mark of her late time as dame in her dwelling, whereby
    I may picture her there;
    And in vain do I urge my unsight
        To conceive my lost prize
At her close, whom I knew when her dreams were
        upbrimming with light,
        And with laughter her eyes.

What scenes spread around her last days,
10   Sad, shining, or dim?
Did her gifts and compassions enray and enarch her sweet
          ways
          With an aureate nimb?
Or did life-light decline from her years,
          And mischances control
Her full day-star; unease, or regret, or forebodings, or fears
          Disennoble her soul?

Thus I do but the phantom retain
          Of the maiden of yore
As my relic; yet haply the best of her – fined in my brain
20   It may be the more
That no line of her writing have I,
          Nor a thread of her hair,
No mark of her late time as dame in her dwelling, whereby
          I may picture her there.

March 1890

In a Wood

FROM 'THE WOODLANDERS'

Pale beech and pine so blue,
     Set in one clay,
Bough to bough cannot you
     Live out your day?
When the rains skim and skip,
Why mar sweet comradeship,
Blighting with poison-drip
     Neighbourly spray?

Heart-halt and spirit-lame,
10   City-opprest,
Unto this wood I came
     As to a nest;

Dreaming that sylvan peace
Offered the harrowed ease –
Nature a soft release
    From men's unrest.

But, having entered in,
    Great growths and small
Show them to men akin –
    Combatants all!   20
Sycamore shoulders oak,
Bines the slim sapling yoke,
Ivy-spun halters choke
    Elms stout and tall.

Touches from ash, O wych,
    Sting you like scorn!
You, too, brave hollies, twitch
    Sidelong from thorn.
Even the rank poplars bear
Lothly a rival's air,   30
Cankering in black despair
    If overborne.

Since, then, no grace I find
    Taught me of trees,
Turn I back to my kind,
    Worthy as these.
There at least smiles abound,
There discourse trills around,
There, now and then, are found
    Life-loyalties.   40

1887: 1896

'I Look Into My Glass'

I look into my glass,
And view my wasting skin,
And say, 'Would God it came to pass
My heart had shrunk as thin!'

For then, I, undistrest
By hearts grown cold to me,
Could lonely wait my endless rest
With equanimity.

But Time, to make me grieve,
Part steals, lets part abide;
And shakes this fragile frame at eve
With throbbings of noontide.

From *Poems of the Past and the Present*
(1901)

Drummer Hodge

I

They throw in Drummer Hodge, to rest
  Uncoffined – just as found:
His landmark is a kopje-crest
  That breaks the veldt around;
And foreign constellations west
  Each night above his mound.

II

Young Hodge the Drummer never knew –
  Fresh from his Wessex home –
The meaning of the broad Karoo,
  The Bush, the dusty loam,
And why uprose to nightly view
  Strange stars amid the gloam.

III

Yet portion of that unknown plain
  Will Hodge for ever be;
His homely Northern breast and brain
  Grow to some Southern tree,
And strange-eyed constellations reign
  His stars eternally.

10

A Wife in London

(December 1899)

I

She sits in the tawny vapour
   That the Thames-side lanes have uprolled,
   Behind whose webby fold on fold
Like a waning taper
   The street-lamp glimmers cold.

A messenger's knock cracks smartly,
   Flashed news is in her hand
   Of meaning it dazes to understand
Though shaped so shortly:
10   *He – has fallen – in the far South Land* . . .

II

'Tis the morrow; the fog hangs thicker,
   The postman nears and goes:
   A letter is brought whose lines disclose
By the firelight flicker
   His hand, whom the worm now knows:

Fresh – firm – penned in highest feather –
   Page-full of his hoped return,
   And of home-planned jaunts by brake and burn
In the summer weather,
20   And of new love that they would learn.

The Souls of the Slain

I

The thick lids of Night closed upon me
   Alone at the Bill
   Of the Isle by the Race –
Many-caverned, bald, wrinkled of face –
And with darkness and silence the spirit was on me
   To brood and be still.

II

No wind fanned the flats of the ocean,
    Or promontory sides,
    Or the ooze by the strand,
    Or the bent-bearded slope of the land,   10
Whose base took its rest amid everlong motion
    Of criss-crossing tides.

III

Soon from out of the Southward seemed nearing
    A whirr, as of wings
    Waved by mighty-vanned flies,
    Or by night-moths of measureless size,
And in softness and smoothness well-nigh beyond hearing
    Of corporal things.

IV

And they bore to the bluff, and alighted –
    A dim-discerned train   20
    Of sprites without mould,
    Frameless souls none might touch or might hold –
On the ledge by the turreted lantern, far-sighted
    By men of the main.

V

And I heard them say 'Home!' and I knew them
    For souls of the felled
    On the earth's nether bord
    Under Capricorn, whither they'd warred,
And I neared in my awe, and gave heedfulness to them
    With breathings inheld.   30

VI

Then, it seemed, there approached from the
        northward
    A senior soul-flame
    Of the like filmy hue:
    And he met them and spake: 'Is it you,
O my men?' Said they, 'Aye! We bear homeward and
        hearthward
    To feast on our fame!'

VII

'I've flown there before you,' he said then:
'Your households are well;
But – your kin linger less
On your glory and war-mightiness
Than on dearer things.' – 'Dearer?' cried these from the
dead then,
'Of what do they tell?'

VIII

'Some mothers muse sadly, and murmur
Your doings as boys –
Recall the quaint ways
Of your babyhood's innocent days.
Some pray that, ere dying, your faith had grown firmer,
And higher your joys.

IX

'A father broods: "Would I had set him
To some humble trade,
And so slacked his high fire,
And his passionate martial desire;
And told him no stories to woo him and whet him
To this dire crusade!"'

X

'And, General, how hold out our sweethearts,
Sworn loyal as doves?'
– 'Many mourn; many think
It is not unattractive to prink
Them in sables for heroes. Some fickle and fleet hearts
Have found them new loves.'

XI

'And our wives?' quoth another resignedly,
'Dwell they on our deeds?'
– 'Deeds of home; that live yet
Fresh as new – deeds of fondness or fret;
Ancient words that were kindly expressed or unkindly,
These, these have their heeds.'

XII

– 'Alas! then it seems that our glory
 Weighs less in their thought
 Than our old homely acts,
And the long-ago commonplace facts   70
Of our lives – held by us as scarce part of our story,
 And rated as nought!'

XIII

Then bitterly some: 'Was it wise now
 To raise the tomb–door
 For such knowledge? Away!'
But the rest: 'Fame we prized till to-day;
Yet that hearts keep us green for old kindness we prize
   now
 A thousand times more!'

XIV

Thus speaking, the trooped apparitions
 Began to disband   80
 And resolve them in two:
Those whose record was lovely and true
Bore to northward for home: those of bitter traditions
 Again left the land,

XV

And, towering to seaward in legions,
 They paused at a spot
 Overbending the Race –
That engulphing, ghast, sinister place –
Whither headlong they plunged, to the fathomless regions
 Of myriads forgot.   90

XVI

And the spirits of those who were homing
 Passed on, rushingly,
 Like the Pentecost Wind;
And the whirr of their wayfaring thinned
And surceased on the sky, and but left in the gloaming
 Sea-mutterings and me.

December 1899

Shelley's Skylark

(*The neighbourhood of Leghorn: March 1887*)

Somewhere afield here something lies
In Earth's oblivious eyeless trust
That moved a poet to prophecies –
A pinch of unseen, unguarded dust:

The dust of the lark that Shelley heard,
And made immortal through times to be; –
Though it only lived like another bird,
And knew not its immortality:

Lived its meek life; then, one day, fell –
10   A little ball of feather and bone;
And how it perished, when piped farewell,
And where it wastes, are alike unknown.

Maybe it rests in the loam I view,
Maybe it throbs in a myrtle's green,
Maybe it sleeps in the coming hue
Of a grape on the slopes of yon inland scene.

Go find it, faeries, go and find
That tiny pinch of priceless dust,
And bring a casket silver-lined,
20   And framed of gold that gems encrust;

And we will lay it safe therein,
And consecrate it to endless time;
For it inspired a bard to win
Ecstatic heights in thought and rhyme.

Rome: At the Pyramid of Cestius near the Graves of Shelley and Keats

(1887)

Who, then, was Cestius,
    And what is he to me? –
Amid thick thoughts and memories multitudinous
    One thought alone brings he.

I can recall no word
    Of anything he did;
For me he is a man who died and was interred
    To leave a pyramid

Whose purpose was exprest
    Not with its first design,   10
Nor till, far down in Time, beside it found their rest
    Two countrymen of mine.

Cestius in life, maybe,
    Slew, breathed out threatening;
I know not. This I know: in death all silently
    He does a finer thing,

In beckoning pilgrim feet
    With marble finger high
To where, by shadowy wall and history-haunted street,
    Those matchless singers lie . . .   20

– Say, then, he lived and died
    That stones which bear his name
Should mark, through Time, where two immortal Shades
            abide;
    It is an ample fame.

The Subalterns

I

'Poor wanderer,' said the leaden sky,
    'I fain would lighten thee,
But there are laws in force on high
    Which say it must not be.'

II

– 'I would not freeze thee, shorn one,' cried
    The North, 'knew I but how
To warm my breath, to slack my stride;
    But I am ruled as thou.'

III

– 'To-morrow I attack thee, wight,'
    Said Sickness. 'Yet I swear
I bear thy little ark no spite,
    But am bid enter there.'

IV

– 'Come hither, Son,' I heard Death say;
    'I did not will a grave
Should end thy pilgrimage to-day,
    But I, too, am a slave!'

V

We smiled upon each other then,
    And life to me had less
Of that fell look it wore ere when
    They owned their passiveness.

To Lizbie Browne

I

Dear Lizbie Browne,
Where are you now?
In sun, in rain? –

Or is your brow
Past joy, past pain,
Dear Lizbie Browne?

II

Sweet Lizbie Browne,
How you could smile,
How you could sing! –
How archly wile   10
In glance-giving,
Sweet Lizbie Browne!

III

And, Lizbie Browne,
Who else had hair
Bay-red as yours,
Or flesh so fair
Bred out of doors,
Sweet Lizbie Browne?

IV

When, Lizbie Browne,
You had just begun   20
To be endeared
By stealth to one,
You disappeared
My Lizbie Browne!

V

Ay, Lizbie Browne,
So swift your life,
And mine so slow,
You were a wife
Ere I could show
Love, Lizbie Browne.   30

VI

Still, Lizbie Browne,
You won, they said,
The best of men

When you were wed . . .
Where went you then,
O Lizbie Browne?

VII

Dear Lizbie Browne,
I should have thought,
'Girls ripen fast,'
And coaxed and caught
You ere you passed,
Dear Lizbie Browne!

VIII

But, Lizbie Browne,
I let you slip;
Shaped not a sign;
Touched never your lip
With lip of mine,
Lost Lizbie Browne!

IX

So, Lizbie Browne,
When on a day
Men speak of me
As not, you'll say,
'And who was he?' –
Yes, Lizbie Browne!

A Broken Appointment

You did not come,
And marching Time drew on, and wore me numb. –
Yet less for loss of your dear presence there
Than that I thus found lacking in your make
That high compassion which can overbear
Reluctance for pure lovingkindness' sake
Grieved I, when, as the hope-hour stroked its sum,
You did not come.

You love not me,
And love alone can lend you loyalty;   10
– I know and knew it. But, unto the store
Of human deeds divine in all but name,
Was it not worth a little hour or more
To add yet this: Once you, a woman, came
To soothe a time-torn man; even though it be
You love not me?

Birds at Winter Nightfall

(*Triolet*)

Around the house the flakes fly faster,
And all the berries now are gone
From holly and cotonea-aster
Around the house. The flakes fly! – faster
Shutting indoors that crumb-outcaster
We used to see upon the lawn
Around the house. The flakes fly faster,
And all the berries now are gone!

MAX GATE

The Darkling Thrush

I leant upon a coppice gate
    When Frost was spectre-gray,
And Winter's dregs made desolate
    The weakening eye of day.
The tangled bine-stems scored the sky
    Like strings of broken lyres,
And all mankind that haunted nigh
    Had sought their household fires.

The land's sharp features seemed to be
10   The Century's corpse outleant,
His crypt the cloudy canopy,
      The wind his death-lament.
The ancient pulse of germ and birth
      Was shrunken hard and dry,
And every spirit upon earth
      Seemed fervourless as I.

At once a voice arose among
      The bleak twigs overhead
In a full-hearted evensong
20   Of joy illimited;
An aged thrush, frail, gaunt, and small,
      In blast-beruffled plume,
Had chosen thus to fling his soul
      Upon the growing gloom.

So little cause for carolings
      Of such ecstatic sound
Was written on terrestrial things
      Afar or nigh around,
That I could think there trembled through
30   His happy good-night air
Some blessed Hope, whereof he knew
      And I was unaware.

December 1900

The Ruined Maid

C 'O 'melia, my dear, this does everything crown!
Who could have supposed I should meet you in Town?
And whence such fair garments, such prosperi-ty?' –
ᶠ 'O didn't you know I'd been ruined?' said she.

- 'You left us in tatters, without shoes or socks,
  Tired of digging potatoes, and spudding up docks;
  And now you've gay bracelets and bright feathers three!' –
  'Yes: that's how we dress when we're ruined,' said she.

–'At home in the barton you said "thee" and "thou",
  And "thik oon", and "theäs oon", and "t'other"; but now   10
  Your talking quite fits 'ee for high compa-ny!' –
  'Some polish is gained with one's ruin,' said she.

- 'Your hands were like paws then, your face blue and
                                bleak
  But now I'm bewitched by your delicate cheek,
  And your little gloves fit as on any la-dy!' –
  'We never do work when we're ruined,' said she.

- 'You used to call home-life a hag-ridden dream,
  And you'd sigh, and you'd sock; but at present you seem
  To know not of megrims or melancho-ly!' –
  'True. One's pretty lively when ruined,' said she.   20

- 'I wish I had feathers, a fine sweeping gown,
  And a delicate face, and could strut about Town!' –
  'My dear – a raw country girl, such as you be,
  Cannot quite expect that. You ain't ruined,' said she.

WESTBOURNE PARK VILLAS, 1866

The Self-Unseeing

Here is the ancient floor,
Footworn and hollowed and thin,
Here was the former door
Where the dead feet walked in.

She sat here in her chair,
Smiling into the fire;
He who played stood there,
Bowing it higher and higher.

Childlike, I danced in a dream;
10   Blessings emblazoned that day;
Everything glowed with a gleam;
Yet we were looking away!

In Tenebris I

'Percussus sum sicut foenum, et aruit cor meum.' – Ps. ci.

Wintertime nighs;
But my bereavement-pain
It cannot bring again:
Twice no one dies.

Flower-petals flee;
But, since it once hath been,
No more that severing scene
Can harrow me.

Birds faint in dread:
10   I shall not lose old strength
In the lone frost's black length:
Strength long since fled!

Leaves freeze to dun;
But friends can not turn cold
This season as of old
For him with none.

Tempests may scath;
But love can not make smart
Again this year his heart
20   Who no heart hath.

Black is night's cope;
But death will not appal
One who, past doubtings all,
Waits in unhope.

In Tenebris II

*'Considerabam ad dexteram, et videbam; et non erat qui cognosceret me
. . . Non est qui requirat animam meam.'* – Ps. cxli.

When the clouds' swoln bosoms echo back the shouts of
    the many and strong
That things are all as they best may be, save a few to be
    right ere long,
And my eyes have not the vision in them to discern what
    to these is so clear,
The blot seems straightway in me alone; one better he were
    not here.

The stout upstanders say, All's well with us: ruers have
    nought to rue!
And what the potent say so oft, can it fail to be somewhat
    true?
Breezily go they, breezily come; their dust smokes around
    their career,
Till I think I am one born out of due time, who has no
    calling here.

Their dawns bring lusty joys, it seems; their evenings all
    that is sweet;
Our times are blessed times, they cry: Life shapes it as is   10
    most meet,
And nothing is much the matter; there are many smiles to
    a tear;
Then what is the matter is *I*, I say. Why should such an
    one be here? . . .

Let him in whose ears the low-voiced Best is killed by the
    clash of the First,
Who holds that if way to the Better there be, it exacts a full
    look at the Worst,
Who feels that delight is a delicate growth cramped by
    crookedness, custom, and fear,
Get him up and be gone as one shaped awry; he disturbs
    the order here.

1895–96

Sapphic Fragment

'Thou shalt be – Nothing.' – Omar Khayyám.
'Tombless, with no remembrance.' – W. Shakespeare.

Dead shalt thou lie; and nought
  Be told of thee or thought,
For thou hast plucked not of the Muses' tree:
    And even in Hades' halls
    Amidst thy fellow-thralls
No friendly shade thy shade shall company!

From Victor Hugo

Child, were I king, I'd yield my royal rule,
  My chariot, sceptre, vassal-service due,
My crown, my porphyry-basined waters cool,
My fleets, whereto the sea is but a pool,
  For a glance from you!

Love, were I God, the earth and its heaving airs,
  Angels, the demons abject under me,
Vast chaos with its teeming womby lairs,
Time, space, all would I give – aye, upper spheres,
10   For a kiss from thee!

From *Time's Laughingstocks and Other Verses* (1909)

A Trampwoman's Tragedy

(182–)

I

From Wynyard's Gap the livelong day,
    The livelong day,
We beat afoot the northward way
    We had travelled times before.
The sun-blaze burning on our backs,
Our shoulders sticking to our packs,
By fosseway, fields, and turnpike tracks
    We skirted sad Sedge-Moor.

II

Full twenty miles we jaunted on,
    We jaunted on, –
My fancy-man, and jeering John,
    And Mother Lee, and I.
And, as the sun drew down to west,
We climbed the toilsome Poldon crest,
And saw, of landskip sights the best,
    The inn that beamed thereby.

III

For months we had padded side by side,
    Ay, side by side
Through the Great Forest, Blackmoor wide,
    And where the Parret ran.
We'd faced the gusts on Mendip ridge,
Had crossed the Yeo unhelped by bridge,
Been stung by every Marshwood midge,
    I and my fancy-man.

IV

Lone inns we loved, my man and I,
      My man and I;
'King's Stag', 'Windwhistle' high and dry,
      'The Horse' on Hintock Green,
The cosy house at Wynyard's Gap,
'The Hut' renowned on Bredy Knap,
And many another wayside tap
      Where folk might sit unseen.

V

Now as we trudged – O deadly day,
      O deadly day! –
I teased my fancy-man in play
      And wanton idleness.
I walked alongside jeering John,
I laid his hand my waist upon;
I would not bend my glances on
      My lover's dark distress.

VI

Thus Poldon top at last we won,
      At last we won,
And gained the inn at sink of sun
      Far-famed as 'Marshal's Elm'.
Beneath us figured tor and lea,
From Mendip to the western sea –
I doubt if finer sight there be
      Within this royal realm.

VII

Inside the settle all a-row –
      All four a-row
We sat, I next to John, to show
      That he had wooed and won.
And then he took me on his knee,
And swore it was his turn to be
My favoured mate, and Mother Lee
      Passed to my former one.

VIII

Then in a voice I had never heard,
    I had never heard,
My only Love to me: 'One word,
    My lady, if you please!   60
Whose is the child you are like to bear? –
His? After all my months o' care?'
God knows 'twas not! But, O despair!
    I nodded – still to tease.

IX

Then up he sprung, and with his knife –
    And with his knife
He let out jeering Johnny's life,
    Yes; there, at set of sun.
The slant ray through the window nigh
Gilded John's blood and glazing eye,   70
Ere scarcely Mother Lee and I
    Knew that the deed was done.

X

The taverns tell the gloomy tale,
    The gloomy tale,
How that at Ivel-chester jail
    My Love, my sweetheart swung;
Though stained till now by no misdeed
Save one horse ta'en in time o' need;
(Blue Jimmy stole right many a steed
    Ere his last fling he flung).   80

XI

Thereaft I walked the world alone,
    Alone, alone!
On his death-day I gave my groan
    And dropt his dead-born child.
'Twas nigh the jail, beneath a tree,
None tending me; for Mother Lee
Had died at Glaston, leaving me
    Unfriended on the wild.

XII

And in the night as I lay weak,
          As I lay weak,
The leaves a-falling on my cheek,
      The red moon low declined –
The ghost of him I'd die to kiss
Rose up and said: 'Ah, tell me this!
Was the child mine, or was it his?
      Speak, that I rest may find!'

XIII

O doubt not but I told him then,
          I told him then,
That I had kept me from all men
      Since we joined lips and swore.
Whereat he smiled, and thinned away
As the wind stirred to call up day . . .
– 'Tis past! And here alone I stray
      Haunting the Western Moor.

NOTES. – 'Windwhistle' (Stanza IV). The highness and dryness of Windwhis-tle Inn was impressed upon the writer two or three years ago, when, after climbing on a hot afternoon to the beautiful spot near which it stands and entering the inn for tea, he was informed by the landlady that none could be had, unless he would fetch water from a valley half a mile off, the house containing not a drop, owing to its situation. However, a tantalizing row of full barrels behind her back testified to a wetness of a certain sort, which was not at that time desired.

'Marshal's Elm' (Stanza VI), so picturesquely situated, is no longer an inn, though the house, or part of it, still remains. It used to exhibit a fine old swinging sign.

'Blue Jimmy' (Stanza X) was a notorious horse-stealer of Wessex in those days, who appropriated more than a hundred horses before he was caught, among others one belonging to a neighbour of the writer's grand-father. He was hanged at the now demolished Ivel-chester or Ilchester jail above mentioned – that building formerly of so many sinister associations in the minds of the local peasantry, and the continual haunt of fever, which at last led to its condemnation. Its site is now an innocent-looking green meadow.

April 1902

A Sunday Morning Tragedy

(circa 186–)

I bore a daughter flower-fair,
In Pydel Vale, alas for me;
I joyed to mother one so rare,
But dead and gone I now would be.

Men looked and loved her as she grew,
And she was won, alas for me;
She told me nothing, but I knew,
And saw that sorrow was to be.

I knew that one had made her thrall,
A thrall to him, alas for me;   10
And then, at last, she told me all,
And wondered what her end would be.

She owned that she had loved too well,
Had loved too well, unhappy she,
And bore a secret time would tell,
Though in her shroud she'd sooner be.

I plodded to her sweetheart's door
In Pydel Vale, alas for me:
I pleaded with him, pleaded sore,
To save her from her misery.   20

He frowned, and swore he could not wed,
Seven times he swore it could not be;
'Poverty's worse than shame,' he said,
Till all my hope went out of me.

'I've packed my traps to sail the main' –
Roughly he spake, alas did he –
'Wessex beholds me not again,
'Tis worse than any jail would be!'

– There was a shepherd whom I knew,
A subtle man, alas for me: 30
I sought him all the pastures through,
Though better I had ceased to be.

I traced him by his lantern light,
And gave him hint, alas for me,
Of how she found her in the plight
That is so scorned in Christendie.

'Is there an herb . . . ?' I asked. 'Or none?'
Yes, thus I asked him desperately.
'– There is,' he said; 'a certain one . . .'
Would he had sworn that none knew he!

'To-morrow I will walk your way,'
He hinted low, alas for me. –
Fieldwards I gazed throughout next day;
Now fields I never more would see!

The sunset-shine, as curfew strook,
As curfew strook beyond the lea,
Lit his white smock and gleaming crook,
While slowly he drew near to me.

He pulled from underneath his smock
The herb I sought, my curse to be –
'At times I use it in my flock,'
He said, and hope waxed strong in me.

''Tis meant to balk ill-motherings' –
(Ill-motherings! Why should they be?) –
'If not, would God have sent such things?'
So spoke the shepherd unto me.

That night I watched the poppling brew,
With bended back and hand on knee:
I stirred it till the dawnlight grew,
And the wind whiffled wailfully.

'This scandal shall be slain,' said I,
'That lours upon her innocency:
I'll give all whispering tongues the lie;' –
But worse than whispers was to be.

'Here's physic for untimely fruit,'
I said to her, alas for me,
Early that morn in fond salute;
And in my grave I now would be.

– Next Sunday came, with sweet church chimes
In Pydel Vale, alas for me: 70
I went into her room betimes;
No more may such a Sunday be!

'Mother, instead of rescue nigh,'
She faintly breathed, alas for me,
'I feel as I were like to die,
And underground soon, soon should be.'

From church that noon the people walked
In twos and threes, alas for me,
Showed their new raiment – smiled and talked,
Though sackcloth-clad I longed to be.   80

Came to my door her lover's friends,
And cheerly cried, alas for me,
'Right glad are we he makes amends,
For never a sweeter bride can be.'

My mouth dried, as 'twere scorched within,
Dried at their words, alas for me:
More and more neighbours crowded in,
(O why should mothers ever be!)

'Ha-ha! Such well-kept news!' laughed they,
Yes – so they laughed, alas for me.   90
'Whose banns were called in church to-day?' –
Christ, how I wished my soul could flee!

'Where is she? O the stealthy miss,'
Still bantered they, alas for me,
'To keep a wedding close as this . . .'
Ay, Fortune worked thus wantonly!

'But you are pale – you did not know?'
They archly asked, alas for me,
I stammered, 'Yes – some days – ago,'
While coffined clay I wished to be.   100

' 'Twas done to please her, we surmise?'
(They spoke quite lightly in their glee)
'Done by him as a fond surprise?'
I thought their words would madden me.

Her lover entered. 'Where's my bird? –
My bird – my flower – my picotee?
First time of asking, soon the third!'
Ah, in my grave I well may be.

To me he whispered: 'Since your call – '
So spoke he then, alas for me –
'I've felt for her, and righted all.'
– I think of it to agony.

'She's faint to-day – tired – nothing more – '
Thus did I lie, alas for me . . .
I called her at her chamber door
As one who scarce had strength to be.

No voice replied. I went within –
O women! scourged the worst are we . . .
I shrieked. The others hastened in
And saw the stroke there dealt on me.

There she lay – silent, breathless, dead,
Stone dead she lay – wronged, sinless she! –
Ghost-white the cheeks once rosy-red:
Death had took her. Death took not me.

I kissed her colding face and hair,
I kissed her corpse – the bride to be! –
My punishment I cannot bear,
But pray God *not* to pity me.

January 1904

The House of Hospitalities

Here we broached the Christmas barrel,
Pushed up the charred log-ends;
Here we sang the Christmas carol,
And called in friends.

Time has tired me since we met here
   When the folk now dead were young,
Since the viands were outset here
     And quaint songs sung.

And the worm has bored the viol
   That used to lead the tune,   10
Rust eaten out the dial
     That struck night's noon.

Now no Christmas brings in neighbours,
   And the New Year comes unlit;
Where we sang the mole now labours,
     And spiders knit.

Yet at midnight if here walking,
   When the moon sheets wall and tree,
I see forms of old time talking,
     Who smile on me.   20

Bereft

  In the black winter morning
No light will be struck near my eyes
While the clock in the stairway is warning
For five, when he used to rise.
      Leave the door unbarred,
      The clock unwound.
      Make my lone bed hard –
      Would 'twere underground!

  When the summer dawns clearly,
And the appletree-tops seem alight,   10
Who will undraw the curtain and cheerly
Call out that the morning is bright?

  When I tarry at market
No form will cross Durnover Lea
In the gathering darkness, to hark at
Grey's Bridge for the pit-pat o' me.

When the supper crock's steaming,
And the time is the time of his tread,
I shall sit by the fire and wait dreaming
In a silence as of the dead.
            Leave the door unbarred,
            The clock unwound,
            Make my lone bed hard –
            Would 'twere underground!

1901

Autumn in King's Hintock Park

Here by the baring bough
    Raking up leaves,
Often I ponder how
    Springtime deceives, –
I, an old woman now,
    Raking up leaves.

Here in the avenue
    Raking up leaves,
Lords' ladies pass in view,
    Until one heaves
Sighs at life's russet hue,
    Raking up leaves!

Just as my shape you see
    Raking up leaves,
I saw, when fresh and free,
    Those memory weaves
Into grey ghosts by me,
    Raking up leaves.

Yet, Dear, though one may sigh,
    Raking up leaves,
New leaves will dance on high –

Earth never grieves! –
Will not, when missed am I
Raking up leaves.

1901

Shut Out That Moon

Close up the casement, draw the blind,
    Shut out that stealing moon,
She wears too much the guise she wore
    Before our lutes were strewn
With years–deep dust, and names we read
    On a white stone were hewn.

Step not out on the dew-dashed lawn
    To view the Lady's Chair,
Immense Orion's glittering form,
    The Less and Greater Bear: 10
Stay in; to such sights we were drawn
    When faded ones were fair.

Brush not the bough for midnight scents
    That come forth lingeringly,
And wake the same sweet sentiments
    They breathed to you and me
When living seemed a laugh, and love
    All it was said to be.

Within the common lamp-lit room
    Prison my eyes and thought;   20
Let dingy details crudely loom,
    Mechanic speech be wrought:
Too fragrant was Life's early bloom,
    Too tart the fruit it brought!

1904

Reminiscences of a Dancing Man

I

Who now remembers Almack's balls –
    Willis's sometime named –
In those two smooth-floored upper halls
    For faded ones so famed?
Where as we trod to trilling sound
The fancied phantoms stood around,
    Or joined us in the maze,
Of the powdered Dears from Georgian years,
Whose dust lay in sightless sealed-up biers,
    The fairest of former days.

II

Who now remembers gay Cremorne,
    And all its jaunty jills,
And those wild whirling figures born
    Of Jullien's grand quadrilles?
With hats on head and morning coats
There footed to his prancing notes
    Our partner-girls and we;
And the gas-jets winked, and the lustres clinked,
And the platform throbbed as with arms enlinked
    We moved to the minstrelsy.

III

Who now recalls those crowded rooms
    Of old yclept 'The Argyle',
Where to the deep Drum-polka's booms
    We hopped in standard style?
Whither have danced those damsels now!
Is Death the partner who doth moue
    Their wormy chaps and bare?
Do their spectres spin like sparks within
The smoky halls of the Prince of Sin
    To a thunderous Jullien air?

On the Departure Platform

We kissed at the barrier; and passing through
She left me, and moment by moment got
Smaller and smaller, until to my view
      She was but a spot;

A wee white spot of muslin fluff
That down the diminishing platform bore
Through hustling crowds of gentle and rough
      To the carriage door.

Under the lamplight's fitful glowers,
Behind dark groups from far and near,   10
Whose interests were apart from ours,
      She would disappear,

Then show again, till I ceased to see
That flexible form, that nebulous white;
And she who was more than my life to me
      Had vanished quite . . .

We have penned new plans since that fair fond day,
And in season she will appear again –
Perhaps in the same soft white array –
      But never as then!   20

– 'And why, young man, must eternally fly
A joy you'll repeat, if you love her well?'
– O friend, nought happens twice thus; why,
      I cannot tell!

'I Say I'll Seek Her'

I say, 'I'll seek her side
   Ere hindrance interposes';
   But eve in midnight closes,
And here I still abide.

When darkness wears I see
    Her sad eyes in a vision;
    They ask, 'What indecision
Detains you, Love, from me? –

'The creaking hinge is oiled,
    I have unbarred the backway,
    But you tread not the trackway;
And shall the thing be spoiled?

'Far cockcrows echo shrill,
    The shadows are abating,
    And I am waiting, waiting;
But O, you tarry still!'

The Night of the Dance

The cold moon hangs to the sky by its horn,
    And centres its gaze on me;
The stars, like eyes in reverie,
Their westering as for a while forborne,
    Quiz downward curiously.

Old Robert draws the backbrand in,
    The green logs steam and spit;
The half-awakened sparrows flit
From the riddled thatch; and owls begin
    To whoo from the gable-slit.

Yes; far and nigh things seem to know
    Sweet scenes are impending here;
That all is prepared; that the hour is near
For welcomes, fellowships, and flow
    Of sally, song, and cheer;

That spigots are pulled and viols strung;
    That soon will arise the sound
Of measures trod to tunes renowned;
That She will return in Love's low tongue
    My vows as we wheel around.

The Ballad-Singer

Sing, Ballad-singer, raise a hearty tune;
Make me forget that there was ever a one
I walked with in the meek light of the moon
    When the day's work was done.

Rhyme, Ballad-rhymer, start a country song;
Make me forget that she whom I loved well
Swore she would love me dearly, love me long,
    Then – what I cannot tell!

Sing, Ballad-singer, from your little book;
Make me forget those heart-breaks, achings, fears;   10
Make me forget her name, her sweet sweet look –
    Make me forget her tears.

Former Beauties

These market-dames, mid-aged, with lips thin-drawn,
    And tissues sere,
Are they the ones we loved in years agone,
    And courted here?

Are these the muslined pink young things to whom
    We vowed and swore
In nooks on summer Sundays by the Froom,
    Or Budmouth shore?

Do they remember those gay tunes we trod
    Clasped on the green;   10
Aye; trod till moonlight set on the beaten sod
    A satin sheen?

They must forget, forget! They cannot know
    What once they were,
Or memory would transfigure them, and show
    Them always fair.

The Inquiry

And are ye one of Hermitage –
Of Hermitage, by Ivel Road,
And do ye know, in Hermitage
A thatch-roofed house where sengreens grow?
And does John Waywood live there still –
He of the name that there abode
When father hurdled on the hill
    Some fifteen years ago?

Does he now speak o' Patty Beech,
The Patty Beech he used to – see,
Or ask at all if Patty Beech
Is known or heard of out this way?
– Ask ever if she's living yet,
And where her present home may be,
And how she bears life's fag and fret
    After so long a day?

In years agone at Hermitage
This faded face was counted fair,
None fairer; and at Hermitage
We swore to wed when he should thrive.
But never a chance had he or I,
And waiting made his wish outwear,
And Time, that dooms man's love to die,
    Preserves a maid's alive.

A Church Romance

(Mellstock: circa 1835)

She turned in the high pew, until her sight
Swept the west gallery, and caught its row
Of music-men with viol, book, and bow
Against the sinking sad tower-window light.

She turned again; and in her pride's despite
One strenuous viol's inspirer seemed to throw
A message from his string to her below,
Which said: 'I claim thee as my own forthright!'

Thus their hearts' bond began, in due time signed.
And long years thence, when Age had scared Romance,   10
At some old attitude of his or glance
That gallery-scene would break upon her mind,
With him as minstrel, ardent, young, and trim,
Bowing 'New Sabbath' or 'Mount Ephraim'.

The Christening

Whose child is this they bring
   Into the aisle? –
At so superb a thing
The congregation smile
And turn their heads awhile.

Its eyes are blue and bright,
   Its cheeks like rose;
Its simple robes unite
Whitest of calicoes
With lawn, and satin bows.   10

A pride in the human race
   At this paragon
Of mortals, lights each face
While the old rite goes on;
But ah, they are shocked anon.

What girl is she who peeps
   From the gallery stair,
Smiles palely, redly weeps,
With feverish furtive air
As though not fitly there?   20

'I am the baby's mother;
    This gem of the race
The decent fain would smother,
And for my deep disgrace
I am bidden to leave the place.'

'Where is the baby's father?' –
    'In the woods afar.
He says there is none he'd rather
Meet under moon or star
Than me, of all that are.

'To clasp me in lovelike weather,
    Wish fixing when,
He says: To be together
At will, just now and then,
Makes him the blest of men;

'But chained and doomed for life
    To slovening
As vulgar man and wife,
He says, is another thing:
Yea: sweet Love's sepulchring!'

1904

After the Last Breath

(*J. H. 1813–1904*)

There's no more to be done, or feared, or hoped;
None now need watch, speak low, and list, and tire;
No irksome crease outsmoothed, no pillow sloped
    Does she require.

Blankly we gaze. We are free to go or stay;
Our morrow's anxious plans have missed their aim;
Whether we leave to-night or wait till day
    Counts as the same.

The lettered vessels of medicaments
Seem asking wherefore we have set them here;   10
Each palliative its silly face presents
    As useless gear.

And yet we feel that something savours well;
We note a numb relief withheld before;
Our well-beloved is prisoner in the cell
    Of Time no more.

We see by littles now the deft achievement
Whereby she has escaped the Wrongers all,
In view of which our momentary bereavement
    Outshapes but small.   20

1904

The Pine Planters

(*Marty South's Reverie*)

I

We work here together
    In blast and breeze;
He fills the earth in,
    I hold the trees.

He does not notice
    That what I do
Keeps me from moving
    And chills me through.

He has seen one fairer
    I feel by his eye,   10
Which skims me as though
    I were not by.

And since she passed here
   He scarce has known
But that the woodland
   Holds him alone.

I have worked here with him
   Since morning shine,
He busy with his thoughts
   And I with mine.

I have helped him so many,
   So many days,
But never win any
   Small word of praise!

Shall I not sigh to him
   That I work on
Glad to be nigh to him
   Though hope is gone?

Nay, though he never
   Knew love like mine,
I'll bear it ever
   And make no sign!

II

From the bundle at hand here
   I take each tree,
And set it to stand, here
   Always to be;
When, in a second,
   As if from fear
Of Life unreckoned
   Beginning here,
It starts a sighing
   Through day and night,
Though while there lying
   'Twas voiceless quite.

It will sigh in the morning,
   Will sigh at noon,
At the winter's warning,
   In wafts of June;
Grieving that never
   Kind Fate decreed   50
It should for ever
   Remain a seed,
And shun the welter
   Of things without,
Unneeding shelter
   From storm and drought.

Thus, all unknowing
   For whom or what
We set it growing
   In this bleak spot,   60
It still will grieve here
   Throughout its time,
Unable to leave here,
   Or change its clime;
Or tell the story
   Of us to-day
When, halt and hoary,
   We pass away.

The Man He Killed

'Had he and I but met
   By some old ancient inn,
We should have sat us down to wet
   Right many a nipperkin!

'But ranged as infantry,
   And staring face to face,
I shot at him as he at me,
   And killed him in his place.

'I shot him dead because –
10   Because he was my foe,
Just so: my foe of course he was;
      That's clear enough; although

'He thought he'd 'list, perhaps,
'Off-hand like – just as I –
Was out of work – had sold his traps –
      No other reason why.

'Yes; quaint and curious war is!
You shoot a fellow down
You'd treat if met where any bar is,
20   Or help to half-a-crown.'

1902

From *Satires of Circumstance, Lyrics and Reveries* (1914)

Channel Firing

That night your great guns, unawares,
Shook all our coffins as we lay,
And broke the chancel window-squares,
We thought it was the Judgment-day

And sat upright. While drearisome
Arose the howl of wakened hounds:
The mouse let fall the altar-crumb,
The worms drew back into the mounds,

The glebe cow drooled. Till God called, 'No;   10
It's gunnery practice out at sea
Just as before you went below;
The world is as it used to be:

'All nations striving strong to make
Red war yet redder. Mad as hatters
They do no more for Christés sake
Than you who are helpless in such matters.

'That this is not the judgment-hour
For some of them's a blessed thing,
For if it were they'd have to scour
Hell's floor for so much threatening . . .   20

'Ha, ha. It will be warmer when
I blow the trumpet (if indeed
I ever do; for you are men,
And rest eternal sorely need).'

So down we lay again. 'I wonder,
Will the world ever saner be,'
Said one, 'than when He sent us under
In our indifferent century!'

And many a skeleton shook his head.
30   'Instead of preaching forty year,'
My neighbour Parson Thirdly said,
'I wish I had stuck to pipes and beer.'

Again the guns disturbed the hour,
Roaring their readiness to avenge,
As far inland as Stourton Tower,
And Camelot, and starlit Stonehenge.

April 1914

message :

The Convergence of the Twain

(*Lines on the loss of the 'Titanic'*)

I

In a solitude of the sea
Deep from human vanity,
And the Pride of Life that planned her, stilly couches she.

II

Steel chambers, late the pyres
Of her salamandrine fires,
Cold currents thrid, and turn to rhythmic tidal lyres.

III

Over the mirrors meant
To glass the opulent
The sea-worm crawls – grotesque, slimed, dumb,
                indifferent.

IV

10   Jewels in joy designed
To ravish the sensuous mind
Lie lightless, all their sparkles bleared and black and blind.

[handwritten margin notes:]
Maiden Voyage
15 Apr. 1 1912
Harland + Wolff
26 m struck
Iceberg
Man – monster of steel
Nature - inscrutable
the inscrutable

V

Dim moon-eyed fishes near
Gaze at the gilded gear
And query: 'What does this vaingloriousness down
            here?' . . .

VI

Well: while was fashioning
This creature of cleaving wing,
The Immanent Will that stirs and urges everything

VII

Prepared a sinister mate
For her – so gaily great –   20
A Shape of Ice, for the time far and dissociate.

VIII

And as the smart ship grew
In stature, grace, and hue,
In shadowy silent distance grew the Iceberg too.

IX

Alien they seemed to be:
No mortal eye could see
The intimate welding of their later history,

X

Or sign that they were bent
By paths coincident
On being anon twin halves of one august event,   30

XI

Till the Spinner of the Years
Said 'Now!' And each one hears,
And consummation comes, and jars two hemispheres.

After the Visit

(To F. E. D.)

Come again to the place
Where your presence was as a leaf that skims
Down a drouthy way whose ascent bedims
    The bloom on the farer's face.

Come again, with the feet
That were light on the green as a thistledown ball,
And those mute ministrations to one and to all
    Beyond a man's saying sweet.

Until then the faint scent
10   Of the bordering flowers swam unheeded away,
And I marked not the charm in the changes of day
    As the cloud-colours came and went.

Through the dark corridors
Your walk was so soundless I did not know
Your form from a phantom's of long ago
    Said to pass on the ancient floors,

Till you drew from the shade,
And I saw the large luminous living eyes
Regard me in fixed inquiring-wise
20   As those of a soul that weighed,

Scarce consciously,
The eternal question of what Life was,
And why we were there, and by whose strange laws
    That which mattered most could not be.

'When I Set Out for Lyonnesse'

(*1870*)

When I set out for Lyonnesse,
   A hundred miles away,
   The rime was on the spray,
And starlight lit my lonesomeness
When I set out for Lyonnesse
   A hundred miles away.

What would bechance at Lyonnesse
   While I should sojourn there
   No prophet durst declare,
Nor did the wisest wizard guess   10
What would bechance at Lyonnesse
   While I should sojourn there.

When I came back from Lyonnesse
   With magic in my eyes,
   All marked with mute surmise
My radiance rare and fathomless,
When I came back from Lyonnesse
   With magic in my eyes!

A Thunderstorm in Town

(*A Reminiscence: 1893*)

She wore a new 'terra-cotta' dress,
And we stayed, because of the pelting storm,
Within the hansom's dry recess,
Though the horse had stopped; yea, motionless
     We sat on, snug and warm.

Then the downpour ceased, to my sharp sad pain
And the glass that had screened our forms before
Flew up, and out she sprang to her door:
I should have kissed her if the rain
      Had lasted a minute more.

'My Spirit Will Not Haunt the Mound'

My spirit will not haunt the mound
      Above my breast,
But travel, memory-possessed,
To where my tremulous being found
      Life largest, best.

My phantom-footed shape will go
      When nightfall grays
Hither and thither along the ways
I and another used to know
      In backward days.

And there you'll find me, if a jot
      You still should care
For me, and for my curious air;
If otherwise, then I shall not,
      For you, be there.

Wessex Heights

(*1896*)

There are some heights in Wessex, shaped as if by a kindly
      hand
For thinking, dreaming, dying on, and at crises when I
      stand,

Say, on Ingpen Beacon eastward, or on Wylls-Neck
        westwardly,
I seem where I was before my birth, and after death may
        be.

In the lowlands I have no comrade, not even the lone
        man's friend –
Her who suffereth long and is kind; accepts what he is too
        weak to mend:
Down there they are dubious and askance; there nobody
        thinks as I,
But mind-chains do not clank where one's next neighbour
        is the sky.

In the towns I am tracked by phantoms having weird
        detective ways –
Shadows of beings who fellowed with myself of earlier   10
        days:
They hang about at places, and they say harsh heavy
        things –
Men with a wintry sneer, and women with tart
        disparagings.

Down there I seem to be false to myself, my simple self
        that was,
And is not now, and I see him watching, wondering what
        crass cause
Can have merged him into such a strange continuator as
        this,
Who yet has something in common with himself, my
        chrysalis.

I cannot go to the great grey Plain; there's a figure against
        the moon,
Nobody sees it but I, and it makes my breast beat out of
        tune;
I cannot go to the tall-spired town, being barred by the
        forms now passed
For everybody but me, in whose long vision they stand   20
        there fast.

There's a ghost at Yell'ham Bottom chiding loud at the fall
    of the night,
There's a ghost in Froom-side Vale, thin lipped and vague,
    in a shroud of white,
There is one in the railway train whenever I do not want it
    near,
I see its profile against the pane, saying what I would not
    hear.

As for one rare fair woman, I am now but a thought of
    hers,
I enter her mind and another thought succeeds me that she
    prefers;
Yet my love for her in its fulness she herself even did not
    know;
Well, time cures hearts of tenderness, and now I can let
    her go.

So I am found on Ingpen Beacon, or on Wylls-Neck to the
    west,
30 Or else on homely Bulbarrow, or little Pilsdon Crest,
Where men have never cared to haunt, nor women have
    walked with me,
And ghosts then keep their distance; and I know some
    liberty.

'Ah, Are You Digging on My Grave?'

'Ah, are you digging on my grave
    My loved one? – planting rue?'
– 'No: yesterday he went to wed
One of the brightest wealth has bred.
"It cannot hurt her now," he said,
    "That I should not be true."'

'Then who is digging on my grave?
    My nearest dearest kin?'
– 'Ah, no: they sit and think, "What use!

What good will planting flowers produce?   10
No tendance of her mound can loose
   Her spirit from Death's gin."'

'But some one digs upon my grave?
   My enemy? – prodding sly?'
– 'Nay: when she heard you had passed the Gate
That shuts on all flesh soon or late,
She thought you no more worth her hate,
   And cares not where you lie.'

'Then, who is digging on my grave?
   Say – since I have not guessed!'   20
– 'O it is I, my mistress dear,
Your little dog, who still lives near,
And much I hope my movements here
   Have not disturbed your rest?'

'Ah, yes! *You* dig upon my grave . . .
   Why flashed it not on me
That one true heart was left behind!
What feeling do we ever find
To equal among human kind
   A dog's fidelity!'   30

'Mistress, I dug upon your grave
   To bury a bone, in case
I should be hungry near this spot
When passing on my daily trot.
I am sorry, but I quite forgot
   It was your resting-place.'

The Year's Awakening

How do you know that the pilgrim track
Along the belting zodiac
Swept by the sun in his seeming rounds
Is traced by now to the Fishes' bounds

And into the Ram, when weeks of cloud
Have wrapt the sky in a clammy shroud,
And never as yet a tint of spring
Has shown in the Earth's apparelling;
  O vespering bird, how do you know,
   How do you know?

How do you know, deep underground,
Hid in your bed from sight and sound,
Without a turn in temperature,
With weather life can scarce endure,
That light has won a fraction's strength,
And day put on some moments' length,
Whereof in merest rote will come,
Weeks hence, mild airs that do not numb;
  O crocus root, how do you know,
   How do you know?

February 1910

Under the Waterfall

'Whenever I plunge my arm, like this,
In a basin of water, I never miss
The sweet sharp sense of a fugitive day
Fetched back from its thickening shroud of gray.
  Hence the only prime
  And real love-rhyme
  That I know by heart,
  And that leaves no smart,
Is the purl of a little valley fall
About three spans wide and two spans tall
Over a table of solid rock,
And into a scoop of the self-same block;
The purl of a runlet that never ceases
In stir of kingdoms, in wars, in peaces;
With a hollow boiling voice it speaks
And has spoken since hills were turfless peaks.'

'And why gives this the only prime
Idea to you of a real love-rhyme?
And why does plunging your arm in a bowl
Full of spring water, bring throbs to your soul?'   20

'Well, under the fall, in a crease of the stone,
Though where precisely none ever has known,
Jammed darkly, nothing to show how prized,
And by now with its smoothness opalized,
> Is a drinking-glass:
> For, down that pass
> My lover and I
> Walked under a sky
Of blue with a leaf-wove awning of green,
In the burn of August, to paint the scene,   30
And we placed our basket of fruit and wine
By the runlet's rim, where we sat to dine;
And when we had drunk from the glass together,
Arched by the oak-copse from the weather,
I held the vessel to rinse in the fall,
Where it slipped, and sank, and was past recall,
Though we stooped and plumbed the little abyss
With long bared arms. There the glass still is.
And, as said, if I thrust my arm below
Cold water in basin or bowl, a throe   40
From the past awakens a sense of that time,
And the glass we used, and the cascade's rhyme.
The basin seems the pool, and its edge
The hard smooth face of the brook-side ledge,
And the leafy pattern of china-ware
The hanging plants that were bathing there.

'By night, by day, when it shines or lours,
There lies intact that chalice of ours,
And its presence adds to the rhyme of love
Persistently sung by the fall above.   50
No lip has touched it since his and mine
In turns therefrom sipped lovers' wine.'

Poems of 1912–13

Veteris vestigia flammae

The Going

Why did you give no hint that night
That quickly after the morrow's dawn,
And calmly, as if indifferent quite,
You would close your term here, up and be gone
      Where I could not follow
      With wing of swallow
To gain one glimpse of you ever anon!

      Never to bid good-bye,
      Or lip me the softest call,
Or utter a wish for a word, while I
Saw morning harden upon the wall,
      Unmoved, unknowing
      That your great going
Had place that moment, and altered all.

Why do you make me leave the house
And think for a breath it is you I see
At the end of the alley of bending boughs
Where so often at dusk you used to be;
      Till in darkening dankness
      The yawning blankness
Of the perspective sickens me!

      You were she who abode
      By those red-veined rocks far West,
You were the swan-necked one who rode
Along the beetling Beeny Crest,
      And, reining nigh me,
      Would muse and eye me,
While Life unrolled us its very best.

Why, then, latterly did we not speak,
Did we not think of those days long dead,   30
And ere your vanishing strive to seek
That time's renewal? We might have said,
　　　'In this bright spring weather
　　　We'll visit together
Those places that once we visited.'

　　　Well, well! All's past amend,
　　　Unchangeable. It must go.
I seem but a dead man held on end
To sink down soon . . . O you could not know
　　　That such swift fleeing   40
　　　No soul foreseeing –
Not even I – would undo me so!

December 1912

Your Last Drive

Here by the moorway you returned,
And saw the borough lights ahead
That lit your face – all undiscerned
To be in a week the face of the dead,
And you told of the charm of that haloed view
That never again would beam on you.

And on your left you passed the spot
Where eight days later you were to lie,
And be spoken of as one who was not;
Beholding it with a heedless eye   10
As alien from you, though under its tree
You soon would halt everlastingly.

I drove not with you . . . Yet had I sat
At your side that eve I should not have seen
That the countenance I was glancing at

Had a last-time look in the flickering sheen,
Nor have read the writing upon your face,
'I go hence soon to my resting-place;

'You may miss me then. But I shall not know
20   How many times you visit me there,
Or what your thoughts are, or if you go
There never at all. And I shall not care.
Should you censure me I shall take no heed,
And even your praises no more shall need.'

True: never you'll know. And you will not mind.
But shall I then slight you because of such?
Dear ghost, in the past did you ever find
The thought 'What profit,' move me much?
Yet abides the fact, indeed, the same, –
30   You are past love, praise, indifference, blame.

December 1912

The Walk

You did not walk with me
Of late to the hill-top tree
    By the gated ways,
    As in earlier days;
    You were weak and lame,
    So you never came,
And I went alone, and I did not mind,
Not thinking of you as left behind.

I walked up there to-day
10   Just in the former way;
    Surveyed around
    The familiar ground
    By myself again:
    What difference, then?
Only that underlying sense
Of the look of a room on returning thence.

Rain on a Grave

Clouds spout upon her
    Their waters amain
    In ruthless disdain, –
Her who but lately
    Had shivered with pain
As at touch of dishonour
If there had lit on her
So coldly, so straightly
    Such arrows of rain:

One who to shelter
    Her delicate head
Would quicken and quicken
    Each tentative tread
If drops chanced to pelt her
    That summertime spills
    In dust-paven rills
When thunder-clouds thicken
    And birds close their bills.

Would that I lay there
    And she were housed here!
Or better, together
Were folded away there
Exposed to one weather
We both, – who would stray there
When sunny the day there,
    Or evening was clear
    At the prime of the year.

Soon will be growing
    Green blades from her mound,
And daisies be showing
    Like stars on the ground,
Till she form part of them –
Ay – the sweet heart of them,

Loved beyond measure
With a child's pleasure
All her life's round.

31 January 1913

'I Found Her Out There'

I found her out there
On a slope few see,
That falls westwardly
To the salt-edged air,
Where the ocean breaks
On the purple strand,
And the hurricane shakes
The solid land.

I brought her here,
And have laid her to rest
In a noiseless nest
No sea beats near.
She will never be stirred
In her loamy cell
By the waves long heard
And loved so well.

So she does not sleep
By those haunted heights
The Atlantic smites
And the blind gales sweep,
Whence she often would gaze
At Dundagel's famed head,
While the dipping blaze
Dyed her face fire-red;

And would sigh at the tale
Of sunk Lyonnesse,
As a wind-tugged tress
Flapped her cheek like a flail;

Or listen at whiles
With a thought-bound brow 30
To the murmuring miles
She is far from now.

Yet her shade, maybe,
Will creep underground
Till it catch the sound
Of that western sea
As it swells and sobs
Where she once domiciled,
And joy in its throbs
With the heart of a child. 40

Without Ceremony

It was your way, my dear,
To vanish without a word
When callers, friends, or kin
Had left, and I hastened in
To rejoin you, as I inferred.

And when you'd a mind to career
Off anywhere – say to town –
You were all on a sudden gone
Before I had thought thereon,
Or noticed your trunks were down. 10

So, now that you disappear
For ever in that swift style,
Your meaning seems to me
Just as it used to be:
'Good-bye is not worth while!'

Lament

How she would have loved
A party to-day! –
Bright-hatted and gloved,
With table and tray
And chairs on the lawn
Her smiles would have shone
With welcomings . . . But
She is shut, she is shut
    From friendship's spell
    In the jailing shell
    Of her tiny cell.

Or she would have reigned
At a dinner to-night
With ardours unfeigned,
And a generous delight:
All in her abode
She'd have freely bestowed
On her guests . . . But alas,
She is shut under grass
    Where no cups flow,
    Powerless to know
    That it might be so.

And she would have sought
With a child's eager glance
The shy snowdrops brought
By the new year's advance,
And peered in the rime
Of Candlemas-time
For crocuses . . . chanced
It that she were not tranced
    From sights she loved best;
    Wholly possessed
    By an infinite rest!

And we are here staying
Amid these stale things,
Who care not for gaying,
And those junketings
That used so to joy her,
And never to cloy her
As us they cloy! . . . But
She is shut, she is shut
    From the cheer of them, dead
    To all done and said
    In her yew-arched bed.

40

The Haunter

He does not think that I haunt here nightly:
    How shall I let him know
That whither his fancy sets him wandering
    I, too, alertly go? –
Hover and hover a few feet from him
    Just as I used to do,
But cannot answer the words he lifts me –
    Only listen thereto!

When I could answer he did not say them:
    – When I could let him know   10
How I would like to join in his journeys
    Seldom he wished to go.
Now that he goes and wants me with him
    More than he used to do,
Never he sees my faithful phantom
    Though he speaks thereto.

Yes, I companion him to places
    Only dreamers know,
Where the shy hares print long paces,
    Where the night rooks go;   20

Into old aisles where the past is all to him,
    Close as his shade can do,
Always lacking the power to call to him,
    Near as I reach thereto!

What a good haunter I am, O tell him!
    Quickly make him know
If he but sigh since my loss befell him
    Straight to his side I go.
Tell him a faithful one is doing
30   All that love can do
Still that his path may be worth pursuing,
    And to bring peace thereto.

The Voice

Woman much missed, how you call to me, call to me,
Saying that now you are not as you were
When you had changed from the one who was all to me,
But as at first, when our day was fair.

Can it be you that I hear? Let me view you, then,
Standing as when I drew near to the town
Where you would wait for me: yes, as I knew you then,
Even to the original air-blue gown!

Or is it only the breeze, in its listlessness
10 Travelling across the wet mead to me here,
You being ever dissolved to wan wistlessness,
Heard no more again far or near?

    Thus I; faltering forward,
    Leaves around me falling,
Wind oozing thin through the thorn from norward,
    And the woman calling.

December 1912

His Visitor

I come across from Mellstock while the moon wastes
             weaker
To behold where I lived with you for twenty years and
             more:
I shall go in the gray, at the passing of the mail-train,
And need no setting open of the long familiar door
             As before.

The change I notice in my once own quarters!
A formal-fashioned border where the daisies used to be,
The rooms new painted, and the pictures altered,
And other cups and saucers, and no cosy nook for tea
             As with me.   10

I discern the dim faces of the sleep-wrapt servants;
They are not those who tended me through feeble hours
             and strong,
But strangers quite, who never knew my rule here,
Who never saw me painting, never heard my softling song
             Float along.

So I don't want to linger in this re-decked dwelling,
I feel too uneasy at the contrasts I behold,
And I make again for Mellstock to return here never,
And rejoin the roomy silence, and the mute and manifold
             Souls of old.   20

1913

A Circular

As 'legal representative'
I read a missive not my own,
On new designs the senders give
    For clothes, in tints as shown.

Here figure blouses, gowns for tea,
And presentation-trains of state,
Charming ball-dresses, millinery,
　　Warranted up to date.

And this gay-pictured, spring-time shout
Of Fashion, hails what lady proud?
Her who before last year ebbed out
　　Was costumed in a shroud.

A Dream or No

Why go to Saint-Juliot? What's Juliot to me?
　　Some strange necromancy
　　But charmed me to fancy
That much of my life claims the spot as its key.

Yes. I have had dreams of that place in the West,
　　And a maiden abiding
　　Thereat as in hiding;
Fair-eyed and white-shouldered, broad-browed and brown-
　　　　tressed.

And of how, coastward bound on a night long ago,
　　There lonely I found her,
　　The sea-birds around her,
And other than nigh things uncaring to know.

So sweet her life there (in my thought has it seemed)
　　That quickly she drew me
　　To take her unto me,
And lodge her long years with me. Such have I dreamed.

But nought of that maid from Saint-Juliot I see;
　　Can she ever have been here,
　　And shed her life's sheen here,
The woman I thought a long housemate with me?

Does there even a place like Saint-Juliot exist?
    Or a Vallency Valley
    With stream and leafed alley,
Or Beeny, or Bos with its flounce flinging mist?

February 1913

After a Journey

Hereto I come to view a voiceless ghost;
    Whither, O whither will its whim now draw me?
Up the cliff, down, till I'm lonely, lost,
    And the unseen waters' ejaculations awe me.
Where you will next be there's no knowing,
    Facing round about me everywhere,
        With your nut-coloured hair,
And gray eyes, and rose-flush coming and going.

Yes: I have re-entered your olden haunts at last;
    Through the years, through the dead scenes I have   10
        tracked you;
What have you now found to say of our past –
    Scanned across the dark space wherein I have lacked
        you?
Summer gave us sweets, but autumn wrought division?
    Things were not lastly as firstly well
        With us twain, you tell?
But all's closed now, despite Time's derision.

I see what you are doing: you are leading me on
    To the spots we knew when we haunted here together,
The waterfall, above which the mist-bow shone
    At the then fair hour in the then fair weather,   20
And the cave just under, with a voice still so hollow
    That it seems to call out to me from forty years ago,
        When you were all aglow,
And not the thin ghost that I now frailly follow!

Ignorant of what there is flitting here to see,
 The waked birds preen and the seals flop lazily,
Soon you will have, Dear, to vanish from me,
 For the stars close their shutters and the dawn whitens
  hazily.
Trust me, I mind not, though Life lours,
30 The bringing me here; nay, bring me here again!
  I am just the same as when
Our days were a joy, and our paths through flowers.

           PENTARGAN BAY

A Death-Day Recalled

Beeny did not quiver,
 Juliot grew not gray,
Thin Valency's river
 Held its wonted way.
Bos seemed not to utter
 Dimmest note of dirge,
Targan mouth a mutter
 To its creamy surge.

Yet though these, unheeding,
10 Listless, passed the hour
Of her spirit's speeding,
 She had, in her flower,
Sought and loved the places–
 Much and often pined
For their lonely faces
 When in towns confined.

Why did not Valency
 In his purl deplore
One whose haunts were whence he
20 Drew his limpid store?

Why did Bos not thunder,
    Targan apprehend
Body and Breath were sunder
    Of their former friend?

Beeny Cliff

MARCH 1870–MARCH 1913

I

O the opal and the sapphire of that wandering western sea,
And the woman riding high above with bright hair flapping
        free –
The woman whom I loved so, and who loyally loved me.

II

The pale mews plained below us, and the waves seemed far
        away
In a nether sky, engrossed in saying their ceaseless babbling
        say,
As we laughed light-heartedly aloft on that clear-sunned
        March day.

III

A little cloud then cloaked us, and there flew an irised rain,
And the Atlantic dyed its levels with a dull misfeatured
        stain,
And then the sun burst out again, and purples prinked the
        main.

IV

– Still in all its chasmal beauty bulks old Beeny to the sky,   10
And shall she and I not go there once again now March is
        nigh,
And the sweet things said in that March say anew there by
        and by?

V

What if still in chasmal beauty looms that wild weird
          western shore,
The woman now is – elsewhere – whom the ambling pony
          bore,
And nor knows nor cares for Beeny, and will laugh there
          nevermore.

At Castle Boterel

As I drive to the junction of lane and highway,
     And the drizzle bedrenches the waggonette,
I look behind at the fading byway,
     And see on its slope, now glistening wet,
          Distinctly yet

Myself and a girlish form benighted
     In dry March weather. We climb the road
Beside a chaise. We had just alighted
     To ease the sturdy pony's load
          When he sighed and slowed.

What we did as we climbed, and what we talked of
     Matters not much, nor to what it led, –
Something that life will not be balked of
     Without rude reason till hope is dead,
          And feeling fled.

It filled but a minute. But was there ever
     A time of such quality, since or before,
In that hill's story? To one mind never,
     Though it has been climbed, foot-swift, foot-sore,
          By thousands more.

Primaeval rocks form the road's steep border,
     And much have they faced there, first and last,
Of the transitory in Earth's long order;
     But what they record in colour and cast
          Is – that we two passed.

And to me, though Time's unflinching rigour,
    In mindless rote, has ruled from sight
The substance now, one phantom figure
    Remains on the slope, as when that night
        Saw us alight.   30

I look and see it there, shrinking, shrinking,
    I look back at it amid the rain
For the very last time; for my sand is sinking,
    And I shall traverse old love's domain
        Never again.

                March 1913

Places

Nobody says: Ah, that is the place
Where chanced, in the hollow of years ago,
What none of the Three Towns cared to know –
The birth of a little girl of grace –
The sweetest the house saw, first or last;
        Yet it was so
        On that day long past.

Nobody thinks: There, there she lay
In a room by the Hoe, like the bud of a flower,
And listened, just after the bedtime hour,   10
To the stammering chimes that used to play
The quaint Old Hundred-and-Thirteenth tune
        In Saint Andrew's tower
        Night, morn, and noon.

Nobody calls to mind that here
Upon Boterel Hill, where the waggoners skid,
With cheeks whose airy flush outbid
Fresh fruit in bloom, and free of fear,
She cantered down, as if she must fall
        (Though she never did),   20
        To the charm of all.

Nay: one there is to whom these things,
That nobody else's mind calls back,
Have a savour that scenes in being lack,
And a presence more than the actual brings;
To whom to-day is beneaped and stale,
And its urgent clack
But a vapid tale.

PLYMOUTH, *March 1913*

The Phantom Horsewoman

I

Queer are the ways of a man I know:
He comes and stands
In a careworn craze,
And looks at the sands
And the seaward haze
With moveless hands
And face and gaze,
Then turns to go . . .
And what does he see when he gazes so?

II

10   They say he sees as an instant thing
More clear than to-day,
A sweet soft scene
That once was in play
By that briny green;
Yes, notes alway
Warm, real, and keen,
What his back years bring –
A phantom of his own figuring.

III

Of this vision of his they might say more:
20   Not only there
Does he see this sight,
But everywhere

In his brain – day, night,
    As if on the air
    It were drawn rose bright –
    Yea, far from that shore
Does he carry this vision of heretofore:

IV

A ghost-girl-rider. And though, toil-tried,
    He withers daily,
    Time touches her not,
    But she still rides gaily
    In his rapt thought
    On that shagged and shaly
    Atlantic spot,
    And as when first eyed
Draws rein and sings to the swing of the tide.

1913

The Spell of the Rose

'I mean to build a hall anon,
    And shape two turrets there,
    And a broad newelled stair,
And a cool well for crystal water;
    Yes; I will build a hall anon,
    Plant roses love shall feed upon,
    And apple-trees and pear.'

He set to build the manor-hall,
    And shaped the turrets there,
    And the broad newelled stair,
And the cool well for crystal water;
    He built for me that manor-hall,
    And planted many trees withal,
    But no rose anywhere.

And as he planted never a rose
    That bears the flower of love,
    Though other flowers throve
Some heart-bane moved our souls to sever
    Since he had planted never a rose;
20   And misconceits raised horrid shows,
    And agonies came thereof.

'I'll mend these miseries,' then said I,
    And so, at dead of night,
    I went and, screened from sight,
That nought should keep our souls in severance,
    I set a rose-bush. 'This,' said I,
    'May end divisions dire and wry,
    And long-drawn days of blight.'

But I was called from earth – yea, called
30   Before my rose-bush grew;
    And would that now I knew
What feels he of the tree I planted,
    And whether, after I was called
    To be a ghost, he, as of old,
    Gave me his heart anew!

Perhaps now blooms that queen of trees
    I set but saw not grow,
    And he, beside its glow –
Eyes couched of the mis-vision that blurred me –
40   Ay, there beside that queen of trees
    He sees me as I was, though sees
    Too late to tell me so!

St Launce's Revisited

    Slip back, Time!
    Yet again I am nearing
    Castle and keep, uprearing
    Gray, as in my prime.

At the inn
Smiling nigh, why is it
Not as on my visit
    When hope and I were twin?

Groom and jade
Whom I found here, moulder;   10
Strange the tavern-holder,
    Strange the tap-maid.

Here I hired
Horse and man for bearing
Me on my wayfaring
    To the door desired.

Evening gloomed
As I journeyed forward
To the faces shoreward,
    Till their dwelling loomed.   20

If again
Towards the Atlantic sea there
I should speed, they'd be there
    Surely now as then? . . .

Why waste thought,
When I know them vanished
Under earth; yea, banished
    Ever into nought!

Where the Picnic Was

Where we made the fire
In the summer time
Of branch and briar
On the hill to the sea,
I slowly climb
Through winter mire,

And scan and trace
The forsaken place
Quite readily.

10   Now a cold wind blows,
And the grass is gray,
But the spot still shows
As a burnt circle – aye,
And stick-ends, charred,
Still strew the sward
Whereon I stand,
Last relic of the band
Who came that day!

Yes, I am here
20   Just as last year,
And the sea breathes brine
From its strange straight line
Up hither, the same
As when we four came.
– But two have wandered far
From this grassy rise
Into urban roar
Where no picnics are,
And one – has shut her eyes
30   For evermore.

[End of *Poems of 1912–13*]

The Newcomer's Wife

He paused on the sill of a door ajar
That screened a lively liquor-bar,
For the name had reached him through the door
Of her he had married the week before.

'We called her the Hack of the Parade;
But she was discreet in the games she played;
If slightly worn, she's pretty yet,
And gossips, after all, forget:

'And he knows nothing of her past;
I am glad the girl's in luck at last;   10
Such ones, though stale to native eyes,
Newcomers snatch at as a prize.'

'Yes, being a stranger he sees her blent
Of all that's fresh and innocent,
Nor dreams how many a love-campaign
She had enjoyed before his reign!'

That night there was the splash of a fall
Over the slimy harbour-wall:
They searched, and at the deepest place
Found him with crabs upon his face.   20

In the Servants' Quarters

'Man, you too, aren't you, one of these rough followers of
          the criminal?
All hanging hereabout to gather how he's going to bear

Examination in the hall.' She flung disdainful glances on
The shabby figure standing at the fire with others there,
    Who warmed them by its flare.

'No indeed, my skipping maiden: I know nothing of the
        trial here,
Or criminal, if so he be. – I chanced to come this way,
And the fire shone out into the dawn, and morning airs are
        cold now;
I, too, was drawn in part by charms I see before me play,
10   That I see not every day.'

'Ha, ha!' then laughed the constables who also stood to
        warm themselves,
The while another maiden scrutinized his features hard,
As the blaze threw into contrast every line and knot that
        wrinkled them,
Exclaiming, 'Why, last night when he was brought in by
        the guard,
        You were with him in the yard!'

'Nay, nay, you teasing wench, I say! You know you speak
        mistakenly.
Cannot a tired pedestrian who has legged it long and far
Here on his way from northern parts, engrossed in humble
        marketings,
Come in and rest awhile, although judicial doings are
20   Afoot by morning star?'

'O, come, come!' laughed the constables. 'Why, man, you
        speak the dialect
He uses in his answers; you can hear him up the stairs.
So own it. We sha'n't hurt ye. There he's speaking now!
        His syllables
Are those you sound yourself when you are talking
        unawares,
        As this pretty girl declares.'

'And you shudder when his chain clinks!' she rejoined. 'O
        yes, I noticed it.
And you winced, too, when those cuffs they gave him
        echoed to us here.

They'll soon be coming down, and you may then have to
    defend yourself
Unless you hold your tongue, or go away and keep you
    clear
    When he's led to judgment near!'   30

'No! I'll be damned in hell if I know anything about the
    man!
No single thing about him more than everybody knows!
Must not I even warm my hands but I am charged with
    blasphemies?' . . .
– His face convulses as the morning cock that moment
    crows,
    And he droops, and turns, and goes.

'Regret Not Me'

    Regret not me;
    Beneath the sunny tree
I lie uncaring, slumbering peacefully.

    Swift as the light
    I flew my faery flight;
Ecstatically I moved, and feared no night.

    I did not know
    That heydays fade and go,
But deemed that what was would be always so.

    I skipped at morn   10
    Between the yellowing corn,
Thinking it good and glorious to be born.

    I ran at eves
    Among the piled-up sheaves,
Dreaming, 'I grieve not, therefore nothing grieves.'

    Now soon will come
    The apple, pear, and plum,
And hinds will sing, and autumn insects hum.

                    Again you will fare
20   To cider-makings rare,
            And junketings; but I shall not be there.

                    Yet gaily sing
                Until the pewter ring
            Those songs we sang when we went gipsying.

                    And lightly dance
                Some triple-timed romance
            In coupled figures, and forget mischance;

                    And mourn not me
                Beneath the yellowing tree;
30   For I shall mind not, slumbering peacefully.

The Recalcitrants

Let us off and search, and find a place
Where yours and mine can be natural lives,
Where no one comes who dissects and dives
And proclaims that ours is a curious case,
Which its touch of romance can scarcely grace.

You would think it strange at first, but then
Everything has been strange in its time.
When some one said on a day of the prime
He would bow to no brazen god again
10 He doubtless dazed the mass of men.

None will see in us a pair whose claims
To righteous judgment we care not making;
Who have doubted if breath be worth the taking,
And have no respect for the current fames
Whence the savour has flown while abide the names.

We have found us already shunned, disdained,
And for re-acceptance have not once striven;
Whatever offence our course has given
The brunt thereof we have long sustained.
20 Well, let us away, scorned, unexplained.

The Sacrilege

A BALLAD-TRAGEDY

(*Circa 182–*)

PART I

'I have a Love I love too well
Where Dunkery frowns on Exon Moor;
I have a Love I love too well,
    To whom, ere she was mine,
"Such is my love for you," I said,
"That you shall have to hood your head
A silken kerchief crimson-red,
    Wove finest of the fine."

'And since this Love, for one mad moon,
On Exon Wild by Dunkery Tor,   10
Since this my Love for one mad moon
    Did clasp me as her king,
I snatched a silk-piece red and rare
From off a stall at Priddy Fair,
For handkerchief to hood her hair
    When we went gallanting.

'Full soon the four weeks neared their end
Where Dunkery frowns on Exon Moor;
And when the four weeks neared their end,
    And their swift sweets outwore,   20
I said, "What shall I do to own
Those beauties bright as tulips blown,
And keep you here with me alone
    As mine for evermore?"

'And as she drowsed within my van
On Exon Wild by Dunkery Tor –
And as she drowsed within my van,
    And dawning turned to day,
She heavily raised her sloe-black eyes

30   And murmured back in softest wise,
        "One more thing, and the charms you prize
            Are yours henceforth for aye.

        '"And swear I will I'll never go
        While Dunkery frowns on Exon Moor
        To meet the Cornish Wrestler Joe
            For dance and dallyings.
        If you'll to yon cathedral shrine,
        And finger from the chest divine
        Treasure to buy me ear-drops fine,
40   And richly jewelled rings."

        'I said: "I am one who has gathered gear
        From Marlbury Downs to Dunkery Tor,
        Who has gathered gear for many a year
            From mansion, mart and fair;
        But at God's house I've stayed my hand,
        Hearing within me some command –
        Curbed by a law not of the land
            From doing damage there!"

        'Whereat she pouts, this Love of mine,
50   As Dunkery pouts to Exon Moor,
        And still she pouts, this Love of mine,
            So cityward I go.
        But ere I start to do the thing,
        And speed my soul's imperilling
        For one who is my ravishing
            And all the joy I know,

        'I come to lay this charge on thee –
        On Exon Wild by Dunkery Tor –
        I come to lay this charge on thee
60   With solemn speech and sign:
        Should things go ill, and my life pay
        For botchery in this rash assay,
        You are to take hers likewise – yea,
            The month the law takes mine.

'For should my rival, Wrestler Joe,
Where Dunkery frowns on Exon Moor –
My reckless rival, Wrestler Joe,
    My Love's bedwinner be,
My rafted spirit would not rest,
But wander weary and distrest   70
Throughout the world in wild protest:
    The thought nigh maddens me!'

PART II

Thus did he speak – this brother of mine –
On Exon Wild by Dunkery Tor,
Born at my birth of mother of mine,
    And forthwith went his way
To dare the deed some coming night . . .
I kept the watch with shaking sight,
The moon at moments breaking bright,
    At others glooming gray.   80

For three full days I heard no sound
Where Dunkery frowns on Exon Moor,
I heard no sound at all around
    Whether his fay prevailed,
Or one more foul the master were,
Till some afoot did tidings bear
How that, for all his practised care,
    He had been caught and jailed.

They had heard a crash when twelve had chimed
By Mendip east of Dunkery Tor,   90
When twelve had chimed and moonlight climbed;
    They watched, and he was tracked
By arch and aisle and saint and knight
Of sculptured stonework sheeted white
In the cathedral's ghostly light,
    And captured in the act.

Yes; for this Love he loved too well
Where Dunkery sights the Severn shore,
All for this Love he loved too well

100   He burst the holy bars,
Seized golden vessels from the chest
To buy her ornaments of the best,
At her ill-witchery's request
        And lure of eyes like stars . . .

When blustering March confused the sky
In Toneborough Town by Exon Moor,
When blustering March confused the sky
        They stretched him; and he died.
Down in the crowd where I, to see
110   The end of him, stood silently,
With a set face he lipped to me –
        'Remember.' 'Ay!' I cried.

By night and day I shadowed her
From Toneborough Deane to Dunkery Tor,
I shadowed her asleep, astir,
        And yet I could not bear –
Till Wrestler Joe anon began
To figure as her chosen man,
And took her to his shining van –
120   To doom a form so fair!

He made it handsome for her sake –
And Dunkery smiled to Exon Moor –
He made it handsome for her sake,
        Painting it out and in;
And on the door of apple-green
A bright brass knocker soon was seen,
And window-curtains white and clean
        For her to sit within.

And all could see she clave to him
130   As cleaves a cloud to Dunkery Tor,
Yea, all could see she clave to him,
        And every day I said,
'A pity it seems to part those two
That hourly grow to love more true:
Yet she's the wanton woman who
        Sent one to swing till dead!'

That blew to blazing all my hate,
While Dunkery frowned on Exon Moor,
And when the river swelled, her fate
   Came to her pitilessly . . .   140
I dogged her, crying: 'Across that plank
They use as bridge to reach yon bank
A coat and hat lie limp and dank;
   Your goodman's, can they be?'

She paled, and went, I close behind –
And Exon frowned to Dunkery Tor,
She went, and I came up behind
   And tipped the plank that bore
Her, fleetly flitting across to eye
What such might bode. She slid awry;   150
And from the current came a cry,
   A gurgle; and no more.

How that befell no mortal knew
From Marlbury Downs to Exon Moor;
No mortal knew that deed undue
   But he who schemed the crime,
Which night still covers . . . But in dream
Those ropes of hair upon the stream
He sees, and he will hear that scream
   Until his judgment-time.   160

Exeunt Omnes

I
   Everybody else, then, going,
And I still left where the fair was? . . .
Much have I seen of neighbour loungers
   Making a lusty showing,
   Each now past all knowing.

II

There is an air of blankness
In the street and the littered spaces;
Thoroughfare, steeple, bridge and highway
    Wizen themselves to lankness;
    Kennels dribble dankness.

III

Folk all fade. And whither,
As I wait alone where the fair was?
Into the clammy and numbing night-fog
    Whence they entered hither.
    Soon one more goes thither!

2 June 1913

In the Study

He enters, and mute on the edge of a chair
Sits a thin-faced lady, a stranger there,
A type of decayed gentility;
And by some small signs he well can guess
That she comes to him almost breakfastless.

'I have called – I hope I do not err –
I am looking for a purchaser
Of some score volumes of the works
Of eminent divines I own, –
Left by my father – though it irks
My patience to offer them.' And she smiles
As if necessity were unknown;
'But the truth of it is that oftenwhiles
I have wished, as I am fond of art,
To make my rooms a little smart,
And these old books are so in the way.'
And lightly still she laughs to him,
As if to sell were a mere gay whim,

And that, to be frank, Life were indeed
To her not vinegar and gall,   20
But fresh and honey-like; and Need
No household skeleton at all.

In the Moonlight

'O lonely workman, standing there
In a dream, why do you stare and stare
At her grave, as no other grave there were?

'If your great gaunt eyes so importune
Her soul by the shine of this corpse-cold moon,
Maybe you'll raise her phantom soon!'

'Why, fool, it is what I would rather see
Than all the living folk there be;
But alas, there is no such joy for me!'

'Ah – she was one you loved, no doubt,   10
Through good and evil, through rain and drought,
And when she passed, all your sun went out?'

'Nay: she was the woman I did not love,
Whom all the others were ranked above,
Whom during her life I thought nothing of.'

From *Moments of Vision and
Miscellaneous Verses* (1917)

'We Sat at the Window'

(*Bournemouth, 1875*)

We sat at the window looking out,
And the rain came down like silken strings
That Swithin's day. Each gutter and spout
Babbled unchecked in the busy way
    Of witless things:
Nothing to read, nothing to see
Seemed in that room for her and me
    On Swithin's day.

We were irked by the scene, by our own selves; yes,
For I did not know, nor did she infer
How much there was to read and guess
By her in me, and to see and crown
    By me in her.
Wasted were two souls in their prime,
And great was the waste, that July time
    When the rain came down.

Afternoon Service at Mellstock

(*Circa 1850*)

On afternoons of drowsy calm
    We stood in the panelled pew,
Singing one-voiced a Tate-and-Brady psalm
    To the tune of 'Cambridge New'.

We watched the elms, we watched the rooks,
  The clouds upon the breeze,
Between the whiles of glancing at our books,
  And swaying like the trees.

So mindless were those outpourings! –
  Though I am not aware
That I have gained by subtle thought on things
  Since we stood psalming there.

In a Museum

I

Here's the mould of a musical bird long passed from light,
Which over the earth before man came was winging;
There's a contralto voice I heard last night,
That lodges in me still with its sweet singing.

II

Such a dream is Time that the coo of this ancient bird
Has perished not, but is blent, or will be blending
Mid visionless wilds of space with the voice that I heard,
In the full-fugued song of the universe unending.

EXETER

At the Word 'Farewell'

She looked like a bird from a cloud
  On the clammy lawn,
Moving alone, bare-browed
  In the dim of dawn.
The candles alight in the room
  For my parting meal
Made all things withoutdoors loom
  Strange, ghostly, unreal.

The hour itself was a ghost,
    And it seemed to me then   10
As of chances the chance furthermost
    I should see her again.
I beheld not where all was so fleet
    That a Plan of the past
Which had ruled us from birthtime to meet
    Was in working at last:

No prelude did I there perceive
    To a drama at all,
Or foreshadow what fortune might weave
    From beginnings so small;   20
But I rose as if quicked by a spur
    I was bound to obey,
And stepped through the casement to her
    Still alone in the gray.

'I am leaving you . . . Farewell!' I said
    As I followed her on
By an alley bare boughs overspread;
    'I soon must be gone!'
Even then the scale might have been turned
    Against love by a feather,   30
– But crimson one cheek of hers burned
    When we came in together.

Heredity

I am the family face;
Flesh perishes, I live on,
Projecting trait and trace
Through time to times anon,
And leaping from place to place
Over oblivion.

The years-heired feature that can
In curve and voice and eye
Despise the human span

10
>Of durance – that is I;
>The eternal thing in man,
>That heeds no call to die.

Near Lanivet, 1872

There was a stunted handpost just on the crest,
    Only a few feet high:
She was tired, and we stopped in the twilight-time for her
        rest,
    At the crossways close thereby.

She leant back, being so weary, against its stem,
    And laid her arms on its own,
Each open palm stretched out to each end of them,
    Her sad face sideways thrown.

Her white-clothed form at this dim-lit cease of day
    Made her look as one crucified
In my gaze at her from the midst of the dusty way,
    And hurriedly 'Don't,' I cried.

I do not think she heard. Loosing thence she said,
    As she stepped forth ready to go,
'I am rested now. – Something strange came into my head;
    I wish I had not leant so!'

And wordless we moved onward down from the hill
    In the west cloud's murked obscure,
And looking back we could see the handpost still
    In the solitude of the moor.

'It struck her too,' I thought, for as if afraid
    She heavily breathed as we trailed;
Till she said, 'I did not think how 'twould look in the
        shade,
    When I leant there like one nailed.'

I, lightly: 'There's nothing in it. For *you*, anyhow!'
   – 'O I know there is not,' said she . . .
'Yet I wonder . . . If no one is bodily crucified now,
   In spirit one may be!'

And we dragged on and on, while we seemed to see
   In the running of Time's far glass   30
Her crucified, as she had wondered if she might be
   Some day. – Alas, alas!

Timing Her

(*Written to an old folk-tune*)

   Lalage's coming:
   Where is she now, O?
   Turning to bow, O,
   And smile, is she,
   Just at parting,
   Parting, parting,
   As she is starting
   To come to me?

   Where is she now, O,
   Now, and now, O,   10
   Shadowing a bough, O,
   Of hedge or tree
   As she is rushing,
   Rushing, rushing,
   Gossamers brushing
   To come to me?

   Lalage's coming;
   Where is she now, O;
   Climbing the brow, O,
   Of hills I see?   20
   Yes, she is nearing,
   Nearing, nearing,
   Weather unfearing
   To come to me.

Near is she now, O,
Now, and now, O;
Milk the rich cow, O,
Forward the tea;
Shake the down bed for her,
Linen sheets spread for her,
Drape round the head for her
Coming to me.

Lalage's coming,
She's nearer now, O,
End anyhow, O,
To-day's husbandry!
Would a gilt chair were mine,
Slippers of vair were mine,
Brushes for hair were mine
Of ivory!

What will she think, O,
She who's so comely,
Viewing how homely
A sort are we!
Nothing resplendent,
No prompt attendant,
Not one dependent
Pertaining to me!

Lalage's coming;
Where is she now, O?
Fain I'd avow, O,
Full honestly
Nought here's enough for her,
All is too rough for her,
Even my love for her
Poor in degree.

She's nearer now, O,
Still nearer now, O,
She it is, I vow, O,
Passing the lea.
Rush down to meet her there,

Call out and greet her there,
Never a sweeter there
Crossed to me!

Lalage's come; aye,
Come is she now, O! . . .
Does Heaven allow, O,
A meeting to be?
Yes, she is here now,
Here now, here now,   70
Nothing to fear now,
Here's Lalage!

The Blinded Bird

So zestfully canst thou sing?
And all this indignity,
With God's consent, on thee!
Blinded ere yet a-wing
By the red-hot needle thou,
I stand and wonder how
So zestfully thou canst sing!

Resenting not such wrong,
Thy grievous pain forgot,
Eternal dark thy lot,   10
Groping thy whole life long,
After that stab of fire;
Enjailed in pitiless wire;
Resenting not such wrong!

Who hath charity? This bird.
Who suffereth long and is kind,
Is not provoked, though blind
And alive ensepulchred?
Who hopeth, endureth all things?
Who thinketh no evil, but sings?   20
Who is divine? This bird.

The Faded Face

How was this I did not see
Such a look as here was shown
Ere its womanhood had blown
Past its first felicity? –
That I did not know you young,
  Faded Face,
    Know you young!

Why did Time so ill bestead
That I heard no voice of yours
Hail from out the curved contours
Of those lips when rosy red;
Weeted not the songs they sung,
  Faded Face,
    Songs they sung!

By these blanchings, blooms of old,
And the relics of your voice –
Leavings rare of rich and choice
From your early tone and mould –
Let me mourn, – aye, sorrow-wrung,
  Faded Face,
    Sorrow-wrung!

Sitting on the Bridge

(*Echo of an old song*)

 Sitting on the bridge
 Past the barracks, town and ridge,
At once the spirit seized us
To sing a song that pleased us –
As 'The Fifth' were much in rumour;
It was 'Whilst I'm in the humour,

Take me, Paddy, will you now?'
And a lancer soon drew nigh,
And his Royal Irish eye
Said, 'Willing, faith, am I,   10
O, to take you anyhow, dears,
To take you anyhow.'

But, lo! – dad walking by,
Cried, 'What, you lightheels! Fie!
Is this the way you roam
And mock the sunset gleam?'
And he marched us straightway home,
Though we said, 'We are only, daddy,
Singing, "Will you take me, Paddy?"'
– Well, we never saw from then,   20
If we sang there anywhen,
The soldier dear again,
Except at night in dream-time,
Except at night in dream.

Perhaps that soldier's fighting
In a land that's far away,
Or he may be idly plighting
Some foreign hussy gay;
Or perhaps his bones are whiting
In the wind to their decay! . . .   30
Ah! – does he mind him how
The girls he saw that day
On the bridge, were sitting singing
At the time of curfew-ringing,
'Take me, Paddy; will you now, dear?
Paddy, will you now?'

GREY'S BRIDGE

The Oxen

Christmas Eve, and twelve of the clock.
　'Now they are all on their knees,'
An elder said as we sat in a flock
　By the embers in hearthside ease.

We pictured the meek mild creatures where
　They dwelt in their strawy pen,
Nor did it occur to one of us there
　To doubt they were kneeling then.

So fair a fancy few would weave
　In these years! Yet, I feel,
If someone said on Christmas Eve,
　'Come; see the oxen kneel,

'In the lonely barton by yonder coomb
　Our childhood used to know,'
I should go with him in the gloom,
　Hoping it might be so.

1915

An Anniversary

It was at the very date to which we have come,
　In the month of the matching name,
When, at a like minute, the sun had upswum,
　Its couch-time at night being the same.
And the same path stretched here that people now
　　　follow,
　And the same stile crossed their way,
And beyond the same green hillock and hollow
　The same horizon lay;
And the same man pilgrims now hereby who pilgrimed
　　　here that day.

Let so much be said of the date-day's sameness;   10
    But the tree that neighbours the track,
And stoops like a pedlar afflicted with lameness,
    Knew of no sogged wound or wind-crack.
And the joints of that wall were not enshrouded
    With mosses of many tones,
And the garth up afar was not overcrowded
    With a multitude of white stones,
And the man's eyes then were not so sunk that you saw the
        socket-bones.

KINGSTON-MAURWARD EWELEASE

Transformations

        Portion of this yew
        Is a man my grandsire knew,
        Bosomed here at its foot:
        This branch may be his wife,
        A ruddy human life
        Now turned to a green shoot.

        These grasses must be made
        Of her who often prayed,
        Last century, for repose;
        And the fair girl long ago   10
        Whom I often tried to know
        May be entering this rose.

        So, they are not underground,
        But as nerves and veins abound
        In the growths of upper air,
        And they feel the sun and rain,
        And the energy again
        That made them what they were!

The Last Signal

(*Oct. 11, 1886*)

A MEMORY OF WILLIAM BARNES

Silently I footed by an uphill road
That led from my abode to a spot yew-boughed;
Yellowly the sun sloped low down to westward,
    And dark was the east with cloud.

Then, amid the shadow of that livid sad east,
Where the light was least, and a gate stood wide,
Something flashed the fire of the sun that was facing it,
    Like a brief blaze on that side.

Looking hard and harder I knew what it meant –
The sudden shine sent from the livid east scene;
It meant the west mirrored by the coffin of my friend
    there,
    Turning to the road from his green,

To take his last journey forth – he who in his prime
Trudged so many a time from that gate athwart the
    land!
Thus a farewell to me he signalled on his grave-way,
    As with a wave of his hand.

WINTERBORNE-CAME PATH

Great Things

Sweet cyder is a great thing,
    A great thing to me,
Spinning down to Weymouth town
    By Ridgway thirstily,
And maid and mistress summoning

Who tend the hostelry:
O cyder is a great thing,
    A great thing to me!

The dance it is a great thing,
    A great thing to me,   10
With candles lit and partners fit
    For night-long revelry;
And going home when day-dawning
    Peeps pale upon the lea:
O dancing is a great thing,
    A great thing to me!

Love is, yea, a great thing,
    A great thing to me,
When, having drawn across the lawn
    In darkness silently,   20
A figure flits like one a-wing
    Out from the nearest tree:
O love is, yes, a great thing,
    A great thing to me!

Will these be always great things,
    Great things to me? . . .
Let it befall that One will call,
    'Soul, I have need of thee':
What then? Joy-jaunts, impassioned flings,
    Love, and its ecstasy,   30
Will always have been great things,
    Great things to me!

Overlooking the River Stour

The swallows flew in the curves of an eight
        Above the river-gleam
        In the wet June's last beam:
Like little crossbows animate
The swallows flew in the curves of an eight
        Above the river-gleam.

Planing up shavings of crystal spray
    A moor-hen darted out
    From the bank thereabout,
And through the stream-shine ripped his way;
Planing up shavings of crystal spray
    A moor-hen darted out.

Closed were the kingcups; and the mead
    Dripped in monotonous green,
    Though the day's morning sheen
Had shown it golden and honeybee'd;
Closed were the kingcups; and the mead
    Dripped in monotonous green.

And never I turned my head, alack,
    While these things met my gaze
    Through the pane's drop-drenched glaze,
To see the more behind my back . . .
O never I turned, but let, alack,
    These less things hold my gaze!

The Musical Box

Lifelong to be
Seemed the fair colour of the time;
That there was standing shadowed near
A spirit who sang to the gentle chime
Of the self-struck notes, I did not hear,
    I did not see.

Thus did it sing
To the mindless lyre that played indoors
As she came to listen for me without:
'O value what the nonce outpours –
This best of life – that shines about
    Your welcoming!'

I had slowed along
After the torrid hours were done,
Though still the posts and walls and road
Flung back their sense of the hot-faced sun,
And had walked by Stourside Mill, where broad
      Stream-lilies throng.

      And I descried
The dusky house that stood apart,   20
And her, white-muslined, waiting there
In the porch with high-expectant heart,
While still the thin mechanic air
      Went on inside.

      At whiles would flit
Swart bats, whose wings, be-webbed and tanned,
Whirred like the wheels of ancient clocks:
She laughed a hailing as she scanned
Me in the gloom, the tuneful box
      Intoning it.   30

      Lifelong to be
I thought it. That there watched hard by
A spirit who sang to the indoor tune,
'O make the most of what is nigh!'
I did not hear in my dull soul-swoon –
      I did not see.

Old Furniture

I know not how it may be with others
    Who sit amid relics of householdry
That date from the days of their mothers' mothers,
    But well I know how it is with me
        Continually.

I see the hands of the generations
   That owned each shiny familiar thing
In play on its knobs and indentations,
   And with its ancient fashioning
     Still dallying:

Hands behind hands, growing paler and paler,
   As in a mirror a candle-flame
Shows images of itself, each frailer
   As it recedes, though the eye may frame
     Its shape the same.

On the clock's dull dial a foggy finger,
   Moving to set the minutes right
With tentative touches that lift and linger
   In the wont of a moth on a summer night,
     Creeps to my sight.

On this old viol, too, fingers are dancing –
   As whilom – just over the strings by the nut,
The tip of a bow receding, advancing
   In airy quivers, as if it would cut
     The plaintive gut.

And I see a face by that box for tinder,
   Glowing forth in fits from the dark,
And fading again, as the linten cinder
   Kindles to red at the flinty spark,
     Or goes out stark.

Well, well. It is best to be up and doing,
   The world has no use for one to-day
Who eyes things thus – no aim pursuing!
   He should not continue in this stay,
     But sink away.

The Last Performance

'I am playing my oldest tunes,' declared she,
    'All the old tunes I know, –
Those I learnt ever so long ago.'
– Why she should think just then she'd play them
    Silence cloaks like snow.

When I returned from the town at nightfall
    Notes continued to pour
As when I had left two hours before:
'It's the very last time,' she said in closing;
    'From now I play no more.'   10

A few morns onward found her fading,
    And, as her life outflew,
I thought of her playing her tunes right through;
And I felt she had known of what was coming,
    And wondered how she knew.

1912

The Interloper

'And I saw the figure and visage of Madness seeking for a home.'

There are three folk driving in a quaint old chaise,
And the cliff-side track looks green and fair;
I view them talking in quiet glee
As they drop down towards the puffins' lair
    By the roughest of ways;
But another with the three rides on, I see,
    Whom I like not to be there!

No: it's not anybody you think of. Next
A dwelling appears by a slow sweet stream
Where two sit happy and half in the dark: 10
They read, helped out by a frail-wick'd gleam,

Some rhythmic text;
But one sits with them whom they don't mark,
    One I'm wishing could not be there.

No: not whom you knew and name. And now
I discern gay diners in a mansion-place,
And the guests dropping wit – pert, prim, or choice,
And the hostess's tender and laughing face,
    And the host's bland brow;
20 But I cannot help hearing a hollow voice,
    And I'd fain not hear it there.

No: it's not from the stranger you met once. Ah,
Yet a goodlier scene than that succeeds;
People on a lawn – quite a crowd of them. Yes,
And they chatter and ramble as fancy leads;
    And they say, 'Hurrah!'
To a blithe speech made; save one, mirthless,
    Who ought not to be there.

Nay: it's not the pale Form your imagings raise,
30 That waits on us all at a destined time,
It is not the Fourth Figure the Furnace showed;
O that it were such a shape sublime
    In these latter days!
It is that under which best lives corrode;
    Would, would it could not be there!

Logs on the Hearth

A MEMORY OF A SISTER

The fire advances along the log
    Of the tree we felled,
Which bloomed and bore striped apples by the peck
    Till its last hour of bearing knelled.

The fork that first my hand would reach
    And then my foot
In climbings upward inch by inch, lies now
    Sawn, sapless, darkening with soot.

Where the bark chars is where, one year,
    It was pruned, and bled –   10
Then overgrew the wound. But now, at last,
    Its growings all have stagnated.

My fellow-climber rises dim
    From her chilly grave –
Just as she was, her foot near mine on the bending limb,
    Laughing, her young brown hand awave.

December 1915

The Sunshade

Ah – it's the skeleton of a lady's sunshade,
    Here at my feet in the hard rock's chink,
    Merely a naked sheaf of wires! –
    Twenty years have gone with their livers and diers
    Since it was silked in its white or pink.

Noonshine riddles the ribs of the sunshade,
    No more a screen from the weakest ray;
    Nothing to tell us the hue of its dyes,
    Nothing but rusty bones as it lies
    In its coffin of stone, unseen till to-day.   10

Where is the woman who carried that sunshade
    Up and down this seaside place? –
    Little thumb standing against its stem,
    Thoughts perhaps bent on a love-stratagem,
    Softening yet more the already soft face!

Is the fair woman who carried that sunshade
A skeleton just as her property is,
Laid in the chink that none may scan?
And does she regret – if regret dust can –
20   The vain things thought when she flourished this?

SWANAGE CLIFFS

The Five Students

The sparrow dips in his wheel-rut bath,
      The sun grows passionate-eyed,
And boils the dew to smoke by the paddock-path;
      As strenuously we stride, –
Five of us; dark He, fair He, dark She, fair She, I,
      All beating by.

The air is shaken, the high-road hot,
      Shadowless swoons the day,
The greens are sobered and cattle at rest; but not
10   We on our urgent way, –
Four of us; fair She, dark She, fair He, I, are there,
      But one – elsewhere.

Autumn moulds the hard fruit mellow,
      And forward still we press
Through moors, briar-meshed plantations, clay-pits
      yellow,
      As in the spring hours – yes,
Three of us; fair He, fair She, I, as heretofore,
      But – fallen one more.

The leaf drops: earthworms draw it in
20   At night-time noiselessly,
The fingers of birch and beech are skeleton-thin,
      And yet on the beat are we, –
Two of us; fair She, I. But no more left to go
      The track we know.

Icicles tag the church-aisle leads,
    The flag-rope gibbers hoarse,
The home-bound foot-folk wrap their snow-flaked
        heads,
    Yet I still stalk the course –
One of us . . . Dark and fair He, dark and fair She, gone:
    The rest – anon.   30

The Wind's Prophecy

I travel on by barren farms,
And gulls glint out like silver flecks
Against a cloud that speaks of wrecks,
And bellies down with black alarms.
I say: 'Thus from my lady's arms
I go; those arms I love the best!'
The wind replies from dip and rise,
'Nay; toward her arms thou journeyest.'

A distant verge morosely gray
Appears, while clots of flying foam   10
Break from its muddy monochrome,
And a light blinks up far away.
I sigh: 'My eyes now as all day
Behold her ebon loops of hair!'
Like bursting bonds the wind responds,
'Nay, wait for tresses flashing fair!'

From tides the lofty coastlands screen
Come smitings like the slam of doors,
Or hammerings on hollow floors,
As the swell cleaves through caves unseen.   20
Say I: 'Though broad this wild terrene,
Her city home is matched of none!'
From the hoarse skies the wind replies:
'Thou shouldst have said her sea-bord one.'

The all-prevailing clouds exclude
The one quick timorous transient star;
The waves outside where breakers are
Huzza like a mad multitude.
'Where the sun ups it, mist-imbued,'
I cry, 'there reigns the star for me!'
The wind outshrieks from points and peaks:
'Here, westward, where it downs, mean ye!'

Yonder the headland, vulturine,
Snores like old Skrymer in his sleep,
And every chasm and every steep
Blackens as wakes each pharos-shine.
'I roam, but one is safely mine,'
I say. 'God grant she stay my own!'
Low laughs the wind as if it grinned:
'Thy Love is one thou'st not yet known.'

Rewritten from an old copy

During Wind and Rain

They sing their dearest songs –
He, she, all of them – yea,
Treble and tenor and bass,
    And one to play;
With the candles mooning each face . . .
    Ah, no; the years O!
How the sick leaves reel down in throngs!

They clear the creeping moss –
Elders and juniors – aye,
Making the pathways neat
    And the garden gay;
And they build a shady seat . . .
    Ah, no; the years, the years;
See, the white storm-birds wing across!

They are blithely breakfasting all –
Men and maidens – yea,
Under the summer tree,
    With a glimpse of the bay,
While pet fowl come to the knee . . .
      Ah, no; the years O!   20
And the rotten rose is ript from the wall.

They change to a high new house,
He, she, all of them – aye,
Clocks and carpets and chairs
    On the lawn all day,
And brightest things that are theirs . . .
      Ah, no; the years, the years;
Down their carved names the rain-drop ploughs.

He Prefers Her Earthly

This after-sunset is a sight for seeing,
Cliff-heads of craggy cloud surrounding it.
   – And dwell you in that glory-show?
You may; for there are strange strange things in being,
    Stranger than I know.

Yet if that chasm of splendour claim your presence
Which glows between the ash cloud and the dun,
   How changed must be your mortal mould!
Changed to a firmament-riding earthless essence
    From what you were of old: 10

All too unlike the fond and fragile creature
Then known to me . . . Well, shall I say it plain?
   I would not have you thus and there,
But still would grieve on, missing you, still feature
    You as the one you were.

'Who's in the Next Room?'

   'Who's in the next room? – who?
     I seemed to see
Somebody in the dawning passing through,
     Unknown to me.'
'Nay: you saw nought. He passed invisibly.'

   'Who's in the next room? – who?
     I seem to hear
Somebody muttering firm in a language new
     That chills the ear.'
10   'No: you catch not his tongue who has entered there.'

   'Who's in the next room? – who?
     I seem to feel
His breath like a clammy draught, as if it drew
     From the Polar Wheel.'
'No: none who breathes at all does the door conceal.'

   'Who's in the next room? – who?
     A figure wan
With a message to one in there of something due?
     Shall I know him anon?'
20   'Yea he; and he brought such; and you'll know him anon.'

The Something That Saved Him

     It was when
Whirls of thick waters laved me
    Again and again,
That something arose and saved me;
     Yea, it was then.

     In that day
Unseeing the azure went I
    On my way,
And to white winter bent I,
10   Knowing no May.

Reft of renown,
Under the night clouds beating
Up and down,
In my needfulness greeting
Cit and clown.

Long there had been
Much of a murky colour
In the scene,
Dull prospects meeting duller;
Nought between.   20

Last, there loomed
A closing-in blind alley,
Though there boomed
A feeble summons to rally
Where it gloomed.

The clock rang;
The hour brought a hand to deliver;
I upsprang,
And looked back at den, ditch and river,
And sang.   30

The Shadow on the Stone

I went by the Druid stone
That broods in the garden white and lone,
And I stopped and looked at the shifting shadows
That at some moments fall thereon
From the tree hard by with a rhythmic swing,
And they shaped in my imagining
To the shade that a well-known head and shoulders
Threw there when she was gardening.

I thought her behind my back,
Yea, her I long had learned to lack,   10
And I said: 'I am sure you are standing behind me,
Though how do you get into this old track?'

And there was no sound but the fall of a leaf
    As a sad response; and to keep down grief
I would not turn my head to discover
    That there was nothing in my belief.

    Yet I wanted to look and see
    That nobody stood at the back of me;
But I thought once more: 'Nay, I'll not unvision
20   A shape which, somehow, there may be.'
    So I went on softly from the glade,
    And left her behind me throwing her shade,
As she were indeed an apparition –
    My head unturned lest my dream should fade.

                    Begun 1913: finished 1916

'For Life I Had Never Cared Greatly'

For Life I had never cared greatly,
    As worth a man's while;
    Peradventures unsought,
    Peradventures that finished in nought,
Had kept me from youth and through manhood till lately
    Unwon by its style.

In earliest years – why I know not –
    I viewed it askance;
    Conditions of doubt,
10   Conditions that leaked slowly out,
May haply have bent me to stand and to show not
    Much zest for its dance.

With symphonies soft and sweet colour
    It courted me then,
    Till evasions seemed wrong,
    Till evasions gave in to its song,
And I warmed, until living aloofly loomed duller
    Than life among men.

Anew I found nought to set eyes on,
    When, lifting its hand,   20
      It uncloaked a star,
    Uncloaked it from fog-damps afar,
And showed its beams burning from pole to horizon
        As bright as a brand.

    And so, the rough highway forgetting,
      I pace hill and dale
      Regarding the sky,
    Regarding the vision on high,
And thus re-illumed have no humour for letting
        My pilgrimage fail.   30

The Pity of It

I walked in loamy Wessex lanes, afar
From rail-track and from highway, and I heard
In field and farmstead many an ancient word
Of local lineage like 'Thu bist', 'Er war',

'Ich woll', 'Er sholl', and by-talk similar,
Nigh as they speak who in this month's moon gird
At England's very loins, thereunto spurred
By gangs whose glory threats and slaughters are.

Then seemed a Heart crying: 'Whosoever they be
At root and bottom of this, who flung this flame   10
Between kin folk kin tongued even as are we,

'Sinister, ugly, lurid, be their fame;
May their familiars grow to shun their name,
And their brood perish everlastingly.'

April 1915

In Time of 'The Breaking of Nations' [1]

I

Only a man harrowing clods
    In a slow silent walk
With an old horse that stumbles and nods
    Half asleep as they stalk.

II

Only thin smoke without flame
    From the heaps of couch-grass;
Yet this will go onward the same
    Though Dynasties pass.

III

Yonder a maid and her wight
    Come whispering by:
War's annals will cloud into night
    Ere their story die.

                                                    1915

[1] Jer. li. 20.

The Coming of the End

How it came to an end!
The meeting afar from the crowd,
And the love-looks and laughters unpenned,
The parting when much was avowed,
    How it came to an end!

It came to an end;
Yes, the outgazing over the stream,
With the sun on each serpentine bend,
Or, later, the luring moon-gleam;
    It came to an end.

It came to an end,
The housebuilding, furnishing, planting,
As if there were ages to spend
In welcoming, feasting, and jaunting;
It came to an end.

It came to an end,
That journey of one day a week:
('It always goes on,' said a friend,
'Just the same in bright weathers or bleak;')
But it came to an end.   20

'*How* will come to an end
This orbit so smoothly begun,
Unless some convulsion attend?'
I often said. 'What will be done
When it comes to an end?'

Well, it came to an end
Quite silently – stopped without jerk;
Better close no prevision could lend;
Working out as One planned it should work
Ere it came to an end.   30

Afterwards

When the Present has latched its postern behind my
                    tremulous stay,
    And the May month flaps its glad green leaves like
                    wings,
Delicate-filmed as new-spun silk, will the neighbours say,
    'He was a man who used to notice such things'?

If it be in the dusk when, like an eyelid's soundless blink,
    The dewfall-hawk comes crossing the shades to alight
Upon the wind-warped upland thorn, a gazer may think,
    'To him this must have been a familiar sight.'

If I pass during some nocturnal blackness, mothy and
          warm,
When the hedgehog travels furtively over the lawn,
One may say, 'He strove that such innocent creatures
          should come to no harm,
    But he could do little for them; and now he is gone.'

If, when hearing that I have been stilled at last, they stand
          at the door,
    Watching the full-starred heavens that winter sees,
Will this thought rise on those who will meet my face no
          more,
    'He was one who had an eye for such mysteries'?

And will any say when my bell of quittance is heard in the
          gloom,
    And a crossing breeze cuts a pause in its outrollings,
Till they rise again, as they were a new bell's boom,
    'He hears it not now, but used to notice such things'?

From *Late Lyrics and Earlier* (1922)

Weathers

I

This is the weather the cuckoo likes,
          And so do I;
When showers betumble the chestnut spikes,
          And nestlings fly:
And the little brown nightingale bills his best,
And they sit outside at 'The Travellers' Rest',
And maids come forth sprig-muslin drest,
And citizens dream of the south and west,
          And so do I.

II

This is the weather the shepherd shuns,
          And so do I;
When beeches drip in browns and duns,
          And thresh, and ply;
And hill-hid tides throb, throe on throe,
And meadow rivulets overflow,
And drops on gate-bars hang in a row,
And rooks in families homeward go,
          And so do I.

Faintheart in a Railway Train

At nine in the morning there passed a church,
At ten there passed me by the sea,
At twelve a town of smoke and smirch,
At two a forest of oak and birch,
          And then, on a platform, she:

A radiant stranger, who saw not me.
I said, 'Get out to her do I dare?'
But I kept my seat in my search for a plea,
And the wheels moved on. O could it but be
10   That I had alighted there!

The Garden Seat

Its former green is blue and thin,
And its once firm legs sink in and in;
Soon it will break down unaware,
Soon it will break down unaware.

At night when reddest flowers are black
Those who once sat thereon come back;
Quite a row of them sitting there,
Quite a row of them sitting there.

With them the seat does not break down,
10   Nor winter freeze them, nor floods drown,
For they are as light as upper air,
They are as light as upper air!

'The Curtains Now Are Drawn'

(Song)

I

The curtains now are drawn,
And the spindrift strikes the glass,
Blown up the jaggèd pass
By the surly salt sou'-west,
And the sneering glare is gone
Behind the yonder crest,
      While she sings to me:

'O the dream that thou art my Love, be it thine,
And the dream that I am thy Love, be it mine,
And death may come, but loving is divine.'   10

II

I stand here in the rain,
With its smite upon her stone,
And the grasses that have grown
Over women, children, men,
And their texts that 'Life is vain';
But I hear the notes as when
    Once she sang to me:
'O the dream that thou art my Love, be it thine,
And the dream that I am thy Love, be it mine,
And death may come, but loving is divine.'   20

1913

Going and Staying

I

The moving sun-shapes on the spray,
The sparkles where the brook was flowing,
Pink faces, plightings, moonlit May,
These were the things we wished would stay;
    But they were going.

II

Seasons of blankness as of snow,
The silent bleed of a world decaying,
The moan of multitudes in woe,
These were the things we wished would go;
    But they were staying.   10

III

Then we looked closelier at Time,
And saw his ghostly arms revolving
To sweep off woeful things with prime,
Things sinister with things sublime
  Alike dissolving.

A Wet August

Nine drops of water bead the jessamine,
And nine-and-ninety smear the stones and tiles:
– 'Twas not so in that August – full-rayed, fine –
When we lived out-of-doors, sang songs, strode miles.

Or was there then no noted radiancy
Of summer? Were dun clouds, a dribbling bough,
Gilt over by the light I bore in me,
And was the waste world just the same as now?

It can have been so: yea, that threatenings
Of coming down-drip on the sunless gray,
By the then golden chances seen in things
Were wrought more bright than brightest skies to-day.

1920

'A Man Was Drawing Near to Me'

On that gray night of mournful drone,
Apart from aught to hear, to see,
I dreamt not that from shires unknown
  In gloom, alone,
  By Halworthy,
A man was drawing near to me.

I'd no concern at anything,
No sense of coming pull-heart play;
Yet, under the silent outspreading
    Of even's wing   10
    Where Otterham lay,
A man was riding up my way.

I thought of nobody – not of one,
But only of trifles – legends, ghosts –
Though, on the moorland dim and dun
    That travellers shun
    About these coasts,
The man had passed Tresparret Posts.

There was no light at all inland,
Only the seaward pharos-fire,   20
Nothing to let me understand
    That hard at hand
    By Hennett Byre
The man was getting nigh and nigher.

There was a rumble at the door,
A draught disturbed the drapery,
And but a minute passed before,
    With gaze that bore
    My destiny,
The man revealed himself to me.   30

The Strange House

(*Max Gate, AD 2000*)

'I hear the piano playing –
    Just as a ghost might play.'
'– O, but what are you saying?
    There's no piano to-day;
Their old one was sold and broken;
    Years past it went amiss.'
'– I heard it, or shouldn't have spoken:
    A strange house, this!

'I catch some undertone here,
   From some one out of sight.'
'– Impossible; we are alone here,
   And shall be through the night.'
'– The parlour-door – what stirred it?'
   '– No one: no soul's in range.'
'– But, anyhow, I heard it,
     And it seems strange!

'Seek my own room I cannot –
   A figure is on the stair!'
'– What figure? Nay, I scan not
     Any one lingering there.
A bough outside is waving,
   And that's its shade by the moon.'
'– Well, all is strange! I am craving
     Strength to leave soon.'

'– Ah, maybe you've some vision
   Of showings beyond our sphere;
Some sight, sense, intuition
   Of what once happened here?
The house is old; they've hinted
     It once held two love-thralls,
And they may have imprinted
     Their dreams on its walls?

'They were – I think 'twas told me –
   Queer in their works and ways;
The teller would often hold me
   With weird tales of those days.
Some folk can not abide here,
   But we – we do not care
Who loved, laughed, wept, or died here,
     Knew joy, or despair.'

A Night in November

I marked when the weather changed,
And the panes began to quake,
And the winds rose up and ranged,
That night, lying half-awake.

Dead leaves blew into my room,
And alighted upon my bed,
And a tree declared to the gloom
Its sorrow that they were shed.

One leaf of them touched my hand,
And I thought that it was you   10
There stood as you used to stand,
And saying at last you knew!

(?) 1913

'And There Was a Great Calm'

(On the Signing of the Armistice, Nov. 11, 1918)

I

There had been years of Passion – scorching, cold,
And much Despair, and Anger heaving high,
Care whitely watching, Sorrows manifold,
Among the young, among the weak and old,
And the pensive Spirit of Pity whispered, 'Why?'

II

Men had not paused to answer. Foes distraught
Pierced the thinned peoples in a brute-like blindness,
Philosophies that sages long had taught,
And Selflessness, were as an unknown thought,
And 'Hell!' and 'Shell!' were yapped at Lovingkindness.   10

III

The feeble folk at home had grown full-used
To 'dug-outs', 'snipers', 'Huns', from the war-adept
In the mornings heard, and at evetides perused;
To day-dreamt men in millions, when they mused –
To nightmare-men in millions when they slept.

IV

Waking to wish existence timeless, null,
Sirius they watched above where armies fell;
He seemed to check his flapping when, in the lull
Of night a boom came thencewise, like the dull
Plunge of a stone dropped into some deep well.

V

So, when old hopes that earth was bettering slowly
Were dead and damned, there sounded 'War is done!'
One morrow. Said the bereft, and meek, and lowly,
'Will men some day be given to grace? yea, wholly,
And in good sooth, as our dreams used to run?'

VI

Breathless they paused. Out there men raised their glance
To where had stood those poplars lank and lopped,
As they had raised it through the four years' dance
Of Death in the now familiar flats of France;
And murmured, 'Strange, this! How? All firing stopped?'

VII

Aye; all was hushed. The about-to-fire fired not,
The aimed-at moved away in trance-lipped song.
One checkless regiment slung a clinching shot
And turned. The Spirit of Irony smirked out, 'What?
Spoil peradventures woven of Rage and Wrong?'

VIII

Thenceforth no flying fires inflamed the gray,
No hurtlings shook the dewdrop from the thorn,
No moan perplexed the mute bird on the spray;
Worn horses mused: 'We are not whipped to-day';
No weft-winged engines blurred the moon's thin horn.

IX

Calm fell. From Heaven distilled a clemency;
There was peace on earth, and silence in the sky;
Some could, some could not, shake off misery:
The Sinister Spirit sneered: 'It had to be!'
And again the Spirit of Pity whispered, 'Why?'

'If It's Ever Spring Again'

(Song)

If it's ever spring again,
  Spring again,
I shall go where went I when
Down the moor-cock splashed, and hen,
Seeing me not, amid their flounder,
Standing with my arm around her;
If it's ever spring again,
  Spring again,
I shall go where went I then.

If it's ever summer-time,   10
  Summer-time,
With the hay crop at the prime,
And the cuckoos – two – in rhyme,
As they used to be, or seemed to,
We shall do as long we've dreamed to,
If it's ever summer-time,
  Summer-time,
With the hay, and bees achime.

The Fallow Deer at the Lonely House

One without looks in to-night
        Through the curtain-chink
From the sheet of glistening white;
One without looks in to-night
        As we sit and think
        By the fender-brink.

We do not discern those eyes
        Watching in the snow;
Lit by lamps of rosy dyes
We do not discern those eyes
        Wondering, aglow,
        Fourfooted, tiptoe.

At Lulworth Cove a Century Back

Had I but lived a hundred years ago
I might have gone, as I have gone this year,
By Warmwell Cross on to a Cove I know,
And Time have placed his finger on me there:

'*You see that man?*' – I might have looked, and said,
'O yes: I see him. One that boat has brought
Which dropped down Channel round Saint Alban's Head.
So commonplace a youth calls not my thought.'

'*You see that man?*' – 'Why yes; I told you; yes:
Of an idling town-sort; thin; hair brown in hue;
And as the evening light scants less and less
He looks up at a star, as many do.'

'*You see that man?*' – 'Nay, leave me!' then I plead,
'I have fifteen miles to vamp across the lea,
And it grows dark, and I am weary-kneed:
I have said the third time; yes, that man I see!'

'Good. That man goes to Rome – to death, despair;
And no one notes him now but you and I:
A hundred years, and the world will follow him there,
And bend with reverence where his ashes lie.'   20

September 1920

NOTE. – In September 1820 Keats, on his way to Rome, landed one day
on the Dorset coast, and composed the sonnet, 'Bright star! would I were
steadfast as thou art.' The spot of his landing is judged to have been
Lulworth Cove.

Evelyn G. of Christminster

I can see the towers
In mind quite clear
Not many hours'
Faring from here;
But how up and go,
And briskly bear
Thither, and know
That you are not there?

Though the birds sing small,
And apple and pear   10
On your trees by the wall
Are ripe and rare,
Though none excel them,
I have no care
To taste them or smell them
And you not there.

Though the College stones
Are stroked with the sun,
And the gownsmen and Dons
Who held you as one   20

Of brightest brow
Still think as they did,
Why haunt with them now
Your candle is hid?

Towards the river
A pealing swells:
They cost me a quiver –
Those prayerful bells!
How go to God,
Who can reprove
With so heavy a rod
As your swift remove!

The chorded keys
Wait all in a row,
And the bellows wheeze
As long ago.
And the psalter lingers,
And organist's chair;
But where are your fingers
That once wagged there?

Shall I then seek
That desert place
This or next week,
And those tracks trace
That fill me with cark
And cloy; nowhere
Being movement or mark
Of you now there!

30

40

Voices from Things Growing in a Churchyard

These flowers are I, poor Fanny Hurd,
     Sir or Madam,
A little girl here sepultured.
Once I flit-fluttered like a bird
Above the grass, as now I wave
In daisy shapes above my grave,
     All day cheerily,
     All night eerily!

– I am one Bachelor Bowring, 'Gent',
     Sir or Madam;   10
In shingled oak my bones were pent;
Hence more than a hundred years I spent
In my feat of change from a coffin-thrall
To a dancer in green as leaves on a wall,
     All day cheerily,
     All night eerily!

– I, these berries of juice and gloss,
     Sir or Madam,
Am clean forgotten as Thomas Voss;
Thin-urned, I have burrowed away from the moss   20
That covers my sod, and have entered this yew,
And turned to clusters ruddy of view,
     All day cheerily,
     All night eerily!

– The Lady Gertrude, proud, high-bred,
     Sir or Madam,
Am I – this laurel that shades your head;
Into its veins I have stilly sped,
And made them of me; and my leaves now shine,
As did my satins superfine,   30
     All day cheerily,
     All night eerily!

- I, who as innocent withwind climb,
      Sir or Madam,
Am one Eve Greensleeves, in olden time
Kissed by men from many a clime,
Beneath sun, stars, in blaze, in breeze,
As now by glowworms and by bees,
      All day cheerily,
40   All night eerily! [1]

- I'm old Squire Audeley Grey, who grew,
      Sir or Madam,
Aweary of life, and in scorn withdrew;
Till anon I clambered up anew
As ivy-green, when my ache was stayed,
And in that attire I have longtime gayed
      All day cheerily,
      All night eerily!

- And so these maskers breathe to each
50   Sir or Madam
Who lingers there, and their lively speech
Affords an interpreter much to teach,
As their murmurous accents seem to come
Thence hitheraround in a radiant hum,
      All day cheerily,
      All night eerily!

[1] It was said her real name was Eve Trevillian or Trevelyan; and that she was the handsome mother of two or three illegitimate children, *circa* 1784-95.

On the Way

The trees fret fitfully and twist,
  Shutters rattle and carpets heave,
  Slime is the dust of yestereve,
    And in the streaming mist
Fishes might seem to fin a passage if they list.

But to his feet,
Drawing nigh and nigher
A hidden seat,
The fog is sweet
And the wind a lyre.   10

A vacant sameness grays the sky,
A moisture gathers on each knop
Of the bramble, rounding to a drop,
    That greets the goer-by
With the cold listless lustre of a dead man's eye.

But to her sight,
Drawing nigh and nigher
Its deep delight,
The fog is bright
And the wind a lyre.   20

'She Did Not Turn'

She did not turn,
But passed foot-faint with averted head
In her gown of green, by the bobbing fern,
Though I leaned over the gate that led
From where we waited with table spread;
    But she did not turn:
Why was she near there if love had fled?

She did not turn,
Though the gate was whence I had often sped
In the mists of morning to meet her, and learn   10
Her heart, when its moving moods I read
As a book – she mine, as she sometimes said;
    But she did not turn,
And passed foot-faint with averted head.

A Two-Years' Idyll

Yes; such it was;
Just those two seasons unsought,
Sweeping like summertide wind on our ways;
Moving, as straws,
Hearts quick as ours in those days;
Going like wind, too, and rated as nought
Save as the prelude to plays
Soon to come – larger, life-fraught:
Yes; such it was.

10
'Nought' it was called,
Even by ourselves – that which springs
Out of the years for all flesh, first or last,
Commonplace, scrawled
Dully on days that go past.
Yet, all the while, it upbore us like wings
Even in hours overcast:
Aye, though this best thing of things,
'Nought' it was called!

What seems it now?
20
Lost: such beginning was all;
Nothing came after: romance straight forsook
Quickly somehow
Life when we sped from our nook,
Primed for new scenes with designs smart and tall . . .
– A preface without any book,
A trumpet uplipped, but no call;
That seems it now.

By Henstridge Cross at the Year's End

(From this centuries-old cross-road the highway leads east to London, north to Bristol and Bath, west to Exeter and the Land's End, and south to the Channel coast.)

Why go the east road now? . . .
That way a youth went on a morrow
After mirth, and he brought back sorrow
Painted upon his brow:
Why go the east road now?

Why go the north road now?
Torn, leaf-strewn, as if scoured by foemen,
Once edging fiefs of my forefolk yeomen,
Fallows fat to the plough:
Why go the north road now?   10

Why go the west road now?
Thence to us came she, bosom-burning,
Welcome with joyousness returning . . .
She sleeps under the bough:
Why go the west road now?

Why go the south road now?
That way marched they some are forgetting,
Stark to the moon left, past regretting
Loves who have falsed their vow . . .
Why go the south road now?   20

Why go any road now?
White stands the handpost for brisk onbearers,
'Halt!' is the word for wan-cheeked farers
Musing on Whither, and How . . .
Why go any road now?

'Yea: we want new feet now'
Answer the stones. 'Want chit-chat, laughter:
Plenty of such to go hereafter
By our tracks, we trow!
30 We are for new feet now.'

During the War

'*If You Had Known*'

If you had known
When listening with her to the far-down moan
Of the white-selvaged and empurpled sea,
And rain came on that did not hinder talk,
Or damp your flashing facile gaiety
In turning home, despite the slow wet walk
By crooked ways, and over stiles of stone:
If you had known

You would lay roses,
10 Fifty years thence, on her monument, that discloses
Its graying shape upon the luxuriant green;
Fifty years thence to an hour, by chance led there,
What might have moved you? – yea, had you foreseen
That on the tomb of the selfsame one, gone where
The dawn of every day is as the close is,
You would lay roses!

1920

Fetching Her

An hour before the dawn,
    My friend,
You lit your waiting bedside-lamp,
    Your breakfast-fire anon,
And outing into the dark and damp
    You saddled, and set on.

Thuswise, before the day,
    My friend,
You sought her on her surfy shore,
    To fetch her thence away   10
Unto your own new-builded door
    For a staunch lifelong stay.

You said: 'It seems to be,
    My friend,
That I were bringing to my place
    The pure brine breeze, the sea,
The mews – all her old sky and space,
    In bringing her with me!'

– But time is prompt to expugn,
    My friend,   20
Such magic-minted conjurings:
    The brought breeze fainted soon,
And then the sense of seamews' wings,
    And the shore's sibilant tune.

So, it had been more due,
    My friend,
Perhaps, had you not pulled this flower
    From the craggy nook it knew,
And set it in an alien bower;
    But left it where it grew!   30

'Could I but Will'

(*Song*: *Verses* 1, 3, *key major*; *verse* 2, *key minor*)

Could I but will,
Will to my bent,
I'd have afar ones near me still,
And music of rare ravishment,
In strains that move the toes and heels!
And when the sweethearts sat for rest
The unbetrothed should foot with zest
Ecstatic reels.

Could I be head,
Head-god, 'Come, now,
Dear girl,' I'd say, 'whose flame is fled,
Who liest with linen-banded brow,
Stirred but by shakes from Earth's deep core –'
I'd say to her: 'Unshroud and meet
That Love who kissed and called thee Sweet! –
Yea, come once more!'

Even half-god power
In spinning dooms
Had I, this frozen scene should flower,
And sand-swept plains and Arctic glooms
Should green them gay with waving leaves,
Mid which old friends and I would walk
With weightless feet and magic talk
Uncounted eves.

Without, Not Within Her

It was what you bore with you, Woman,
Not inly were,
That throned you from all else human,
However fair!

It was that strange freshness you carried
    Into a soul
Whereon no thought of yours tarried
    Two moments at all.

And out from his spirit flew death,
    And bale, and ban,   10
Like the corn-chaff under the breath
    Of the winnowing-fan.

Vagg Hollow

Vagg Hollow is a marshy spot on the old Roman Road near Ilchester, where 'things' are seen. Merchandise was formerly fetched inland from the canal-boats at Load-Bridge by waggons this way.

'What do you see in Vagg Hollow,
Little boy, when you go
In the morning at five on your lonely drive?'
'– I see men's souls, who follow
Till we've passed where the road lies low,
When they vanish at our creaking!

'They are like white faces speaking
Beside and behind the waggon –
One just as father's was when here.
The waggoner drinks from his flagon,   10
(Or he'd flinch when the Hollow is near)
But he does not give me any.

'Sometimes the faces are many;
But I walk along by the horses,
He asleep on the straw as we jog;
And I hear the loud water-courses,
And the drops from the trees in the fog,
And watch till the day is breaking,

'And the wind out by Tintinhull waking;
20   I hear in it father's call
As he called when I saw him dying,
And he sat by the fire last Fall,
And mother stood by sighing;
But I'm not afraid at all!'

First or Last

(Song)

If grief come early
Joy comes late,
If joy come early
Grief will wait;
    Aye, my dear and tender!

Wise ones joy them early
While the cheeks are red,
Banish grief till surly
Time has dulled their dread.

10   And joy being ours
Ere youth has flown,
The later hours
May find us gone;
    Aye, my dear and tender!

The Marble Tablet

There it stands, though alas, what a little of her
    Shows in its cold white look!
Not her glance, glide, or smile; not a tittle of her
    Voice like the purl of a brook;
    Not her thoughts, that you read like a book.

It may stand for her once in November
  When first she breathed, witless of all;
Or in heavy years she would remember
  When circumstance held her in thrall;
  Or at last, when she answered her call!   10

Nothing more. The still marble, date-graven,
  Gives all that it can, tersely lined;
That one has at length found the haven
  Which every one other will find;
  With silence on what shone behind.

ST JULIOT: *8 September 1916*

Last Words to a Dumb Friend

Pet was never mourned as you,
Purrer of the spotless hue,
Plumy tail, and wistful gaze
While you humoured our queer ways,
Or outshrilled your morning call
Up the stairs and through the hall –
Foot suspended in its fall –
While, expectant, you would stand
Arched, to meet the stroking hand;
Till your way you chose to wend   10
Yonder, to your tragic end.

Never another pet for me!
Let your place all vacant be;
Better blankness day by day
Than companion torn away.
Better bid his memory fade,
Better blot each mark he made,
Selfishly escape distress
By contrived forgetfulness,
Than preserve his prints to make   20
Every morn and eve an ache.

From the chair whereon he sat
Sweep his fur, nor wince thereat;
Rake his little pathways out
Mid the bushes roundabout;
Smooth away his talons' mark
From the claw-worn pine-tree bark,
Where he climbed as dusk embrowned,
Waiting us who loitered round.

30 Strange it is this speechless thing,
Subject to our mastering,
Subject for his life and food
To our gift, and time, and mood;
Timid pensioner of us Powers,
His existence ruled by ours,
Should – by crossing at a breath
Into safe and shielded death,
By the merely taking hence
Of his insignificance –
40 Loom as largened to the sense,
Shape as part, above man's will,
Of the Imperturbable.

As a prisoner, flight debarred,
Exercising in a yard,
Still retain I, troubled, shaken,
Mean estate, by him forsaken;
And this home, which scarcely took
Impress from his little look,
By his faring to the Dim
50 Grows all eloquent of him.

Housemate, I can think you still
Bounding to the window-sill,
Over which I vaguely see
Your small mound beneath the tree,
Showing in the autumn shade
That you moulder where you played.

2 October 1904

The Sailor's Mother

'*O whence do you come,*
Figure in the night-fog that chills me numb?'

'I come to you across from my house up there,
And I don't mind the brine-mist clinging to me
      That blows from the quay,
For I heard him in my chamber, and thought you unaware.'

      'But what did you hear,
That brought you blindly knocking in this middle-watch so
          drear?'

'My sailor son's voice as 'twere calling at your door,
And I don't mind my bare feet clammy on the stones,   10
      And the blight to my bones,
For he only knows of *this* house I lived in before.'

      'Nobody's nigh,
Woman like a skeleton, with socket-sunk eye.'

'Ah – nobody's nigh! And my life is drearisome,
And this is the old home we loved in many a day
      Before he went away;
And the salt fog mops me. And nobody's come!'

From 'To Please his Wife'.

Intra Sepulchrum

What curious things we said,
What curious things we did
Up there in the world we walked till dead,
    Our kith and kin amid!

How we played at love,
And its wildness, weakness, woe;
Yes, played thereat far more than enough
    As it turned out, I trow!

                    Played at believing in gods
10   And observing the ordinances,
          I for your sake in impossible codes
                    Right ready to acquiesce.

                    Thinking our lives unique,
                    Quite quainter than usual kinds,
          We held that we could not abide a week
                    The tether of typic minds.

                    – Yet people who day by day
                    Pass by and look at us
          From over the wall in a casual way
20   Are of this unconscious.

                    And feel, if anything,
                    That none can be buried here
          Removed from commonest fashioning,
                    Or lending note to a bier:

                    No twain who in heart-heaves proved
                    Themselves at all adept,
          Who more than many laughed and loved,
                    Who more than many wept,

                    Or were as sprites or elves
30   Into blind matter hurled,
          Or ever could have been to themselves
                    The centre of the world.

The Whitewashed Wall

Why does she turn in that shy soft way
    Whenever she stirs the fire,
And kiss to the chimney-corner wall,
    As if entranced to admire
Its whitewashed bareness more than the sight
    Of a rose in richest green?
I have known her long, but this raptured rite
    I never before have seen.

– Well, once when her son cast his shadow there,
 A friend took a pencil and drew him   10
Upon that flame-lit wall. And the lines
 Had a lifelike semblance to him.
And there long stayed his familiar look;
 But one day, ere she knew,
The whitener came to cleanse the nook,
 And covered the face from view.

'Yes,' he said: 'My brush goes on with a rush,
 And the draught is buried under;
When you have to whiten old cots and brighten,
 What else can you do, I wonder?'   20
But she knows he's there. And when she yearns
 For him, deep in the labouring night,
She sees him as close at hand, and turns
 To him under his sheet of white.

In a London Flat

I

'You look like a widower,' she said
Through the folding-doors with a laugh from the bed,
As he sat by the fire in the outer room,
Reading late on a night of gloom,
And a cab-hack's wheeze, and the clap of its feet
In its breathless pace on the smooth wet street,
Were all that came to them now and then . . .
'You really do!' she quizzed again.

II

And the Spirits behind the curtains heard,
And also laughed, amused at her word,   10
And at her light-hearted view of him.
'Let's get him made so – just for a whim!'
Said the Phantom Ironic. ' 'Twould serve her right
If we coaxed the Will to do it some night.'
'O pray not!' pleaded the younger one,
The Sprite of the Pities. 'She said it in fun!'

III

But so it befell, whatever the cause,
That what she had called him he next year was;
And on such a night, when she lay elsewhere,
He, watched by those Phantoms, again sat there,
And gazed, as if gazing on far faint shores,
At the empty bed through the folding-doors
As he remembered her words; and wept
That she had forgotten them where she slept.

Drawing Details in an Old Church

I hear the bell-rope sawing,
And the oil-less axle grind,
As I sit alone here drawing
What some Gothic brain designed;
And I catch the toll that follows
    From the lagging bell,
Ere it spreads to hills and hollows
    Where people dwell.

I ask not whom it tolls for,
Incurious who he be;
So, some morrow, when those knolls for
One unguessed, sound out for me,
A stranger, loitering under
    In nave or choir,
May think, too, 'Whose, I wonder?'
    But not inquire.

An Ancient to Ancients

Where once we danced, where once we sang,
   Gentlemen,
The floors are sunken, cobwebs hang,
And cracks creep; worms have fed upon
The doors. Yea, sprightlier times were then
Than now, with harps and tabrets gone,
   Gentlemen!

Where once we rowed, where once we sailed,
   Gentlemen,
And damsels took the tiller, veiled   10
Against too strong a stare (God wot
Their fancy, then or anywhen!)
Upon that shore we are clean forgot,
   Gentlemen!

We have lost somewhat, afar and near,
   Gentlemen,
The thinning of our ranks each year
Affords a hint we are nigh undone,
That we shall not be ever again
The marked of many, loved of one,   20
   Gentlemen.

In dance the polka hit our wish,
   Gentlemen,
The paced quadrille, the spry schottische,
'Sir Roger'. – And in opera spheres
The 'Girl' (the famed 'Bohemian'),
And 'Trovatore', held the ears,
   Gentlemen.

This season's paintings do not please,
   Gentlemen,   30
Like Etty, Mulready, Maclise;
Throbbing romance has waned and wanned;
No wizard wields the witching pen
Of Bulwer, Scott, Dumas, and Sand,
   Gentlemen.

The bower we shrined to Tennyson,
> Gentlemen,
Is roof-wrecked; damps there drip upon
Sagged seats, the creeper-nails are rust,
40   The spider is sole denizen;
Even she who voiced those rhymes is dust,
> Gentlemen!

We who met sunrise sanguine-souled,
> Gentlemen,
Are wearing weary. We are old;
These younger press; we feel our rout
Is imminent to Aïdes' den, –
That evening shades are stretching out,
> Gentlemen!

50   And yet, though ours be failing frames,
> Gentlemen,
So were some others' history names,
Who trode their track light-limbed and fast
As these youth, and not alien
From enterprise, to their long last,
> Gentlemen.

Sophocles, Plato, Socrates,
> Gentlemen,
Pythagoras, Thucydides,
60   Herodotus, and Homer, – yea,
Clement, Augustin, Origen,
Burnt brightlier towards their setting-day,
> Gentlemen.

And ye, red-lipped and smooth-browed; list,
> Gentlemen;
Much is there waits you we have missed;
Much lore we leave you worth the knowing,
Much, much has lain outside our ken:
Nay, rush not: time serves: we are going,
70   Gentlemen.

From *Human Shows, Far Phantasies, Songs and Trifles* (1925)

Waiting Both

A star looks down at me,
And says: 'Here I and you
Stand, each in our degree:
What do you mean to do, –
      Mean to do?'

I say: 'For all I know,
Wait, and let Time go by,
Till my change come,' – 'Just so.'
The star says: 'So mean I: –
      So mean I.'   10

A Bird-Scene at a Rural Dwelling

When the inmate stirs, the birds retire discreetly
From the window-ledge, whereon they whistled sweetly
      And on the step of the door,
      In the misty morning hoar;
   But now the dweller is up they flee
   To the crooked neighbouring codlin-tree;
And when he comes fully forth they seek the garden,
And call from the lofty costard, as pleading pardon
      For shouting so near before
      In their joy at being alive: –   10
Meanwhile the hammering clock within goes five.

I know a domicile of brown and green,
Where for a hundred summers there have been
Just such enactments, just such daybreaks seen.

The Later Autumn

Gone are the lovers, under the bush
      Stretched at their ease;
      Gone the bees,
Tangling themselves in your hair as they rush
      On the line of your track,
      Leg-laden, back
      With a dip to their hive
      In a prepossessed dive.

Toadsmeat is mangy, frosted, and sere;
      Apples in grass
      Crunch as we pass,
And rot ere the men who make cyder appear.
      Couch-fires abound
      On fallows around,
      And shades far extend
      Like lives soon to end.

Spinning leaves join the remains shrunk and brown
      Of last year's display
      That lie wasting away,
On whose corpses they earlier as scorners gazed down
      From their aery green height:
      Now in the same plight
      They huddle; while yon
      A robin looks on.

An East-End Curate

A small blind street off East Commercial Road;
    Window, door; window, door;
    Every house like the one before,
Is where the curate, Mr Dowle, has found a pinched
        abode.

Spectacled, pale, moustache straw-coloured, and with a
        long thin face,
Day or dark his lodgings' narrow doorstep does he pace.

A bleached pianoforte, with its drawn silk plaitings faded,
Stands in his room, its keys much yellowed, cyphering, and
        abraded,
'Novello's Anthems' lie at hand, and also a few glees,
And 'Laws of Heaven for Earth' in a frame upon the wall   10
        one sees.

He goes through his neighbours' houses as his own, and
        none regards,
And opens their back-doors offhand, to look for them in
        their yards:
A man is threatening his wife on the other side of the wall,
But the curate lets it pass as knowing the history of it all.

Freely within his hearing the children skip and laugh and
        say:
  'There's Mister Dow-well! There's Mister Dow-well!'
        in their play;
  And the long, pallid, devoted face notes not,
But stoops along abstractedly, for good, or in vain, God
        wot!

The Month's Calendar

Tear off the calendar
Of this month past,
And all its weeks, that are
Flown, to be cast
To oblivion fast!

Darken that day
On which we met,
With its words of gay
Half-felt regret
That you'll forget!   10

The second day, too;
The noon I nursed
Well – thoughts; yes, through
To the thirty-first;
That was the worst.

For then it was
You let me see
There was good cause
Why you could not be
Aught ever to me!

20

When Dead

TO ———

It will be much better when
  I am under the bough;
I shall be more myself, Dear, then,
  Than I am now.

No sign of querulousness
  To wear you out
Shall I show there: strivings and stress
  Be quite without.

This fleeting life-brief blight
  Will have gone past
When I resume my old and right
  Place in the Vast.

10

And when you come to me
  To show you true,
Doubt not I shall infallibly
  Be waiting you.

Night-Time in Mid-Fall

It is a storm-strid night, winds footing swift
    Through the blind profound;
  I know the happenings from their sound;
Leaves totter down still green, and spin and drift;
The tree-trunks rock to their roots, which wrench and lift
The loam where they run onward underground.

The streams are muddy and swollen; eels migrate
    To a new abode;
  Even cross, 'tis said, the turnpike-road;
(Men's feet have felt their crawl, home-coming late):   10
The westward fronts of towers are saturate,
Church-timbers crack, and witches ride abroad.

A Sheep Fair

  The day arrives of the autumn fair,
    And torrents fall,
  Though sheep in throngs are gathered there,
    Ten thousand all,
  Sodden, with hurdles round them reared:
  And, lot by lot, the pens are cleared,
  And the auctioneer wrings out his beard,
  And wipes his book, bedrenched and smeared,
And rakes the rain from his face with the edge of his hand,
    As torrents fall.   10

  The wool of the ewes is like a sponge
    With the daylong rain:
  Jammed tight, to turn, or lie, or lunge,
    They strive in vain.
  Their horns are soft as finger-nails,
  Their shepherds reek against the rails,

The tied dogs soak with tucked-in tails,
The buyers' hat-brims fill like pails,
Which spill small cascades when they shift their stand
20   In the daylong rain.

POSTSCRIPT

Time has trailed lengthily since met
    At Pummery Fair
Those panting thousands in their wet
    And woolly wear:
And every flock long since has bled,
And all the dripping buyers have sped,
And the hoarse auctioneer is dead,
Who 'Going – going!' so often said,
As he consigned to doom each meek, mewed band
30   At Pummery Fair.

Snow in the Suburbs

Every branch big with it,
    Bent every twig with it;
Every fork like a white web-foot;
Every street and pavement mute:
Some flakes have lost their way, and grope back upward,
    when
Meeting those meandering down they turn and descend
    again.
The palings are glued together like a wall,
And there is no waft of wind with the fleecy fall.

A sparrow enters the tree,
10   Whereon immediately
A snow-lump thrice his own slight size
Descends on him and showers his head and eyes,

And overturns him,
And near inurns him,
And lights on a nether twig, when its brush
Starts off a volley of other lodging lumps with a rush.

The steps are a blanched slope,
Up which, with feeble hope,
A black cat comes, wide-eyed and thin;
And we take him in.   20

Ice on the Highway

Seven buxom women abreast, and arm in arm,
Trudge down the hill, tip-toed,
And breathing warm;
They must perforce trudge thus, to keep upright
On the glassy ice-bound road,
And they must get to market whether or no,
Provisions running low
With the nearing Saturday night,
While the lumbering van wherein they mostly ride
Can nowise go: 10
Yet loud their laughter as they stagger and slide!

YELL'HAM HILL

No Buyers

A STREET SCENE

A load of brushes and baskets and cradles and chairs
Labours along the street in the rain:
With it a man, a woman, a pony with whiteybrown hairs. –
The man foots in front of the horse with a shambling
sway
At a slower tread than a funeral train,

While to a dirge-like tune he chants his wares,
Swinging a Turk's-head brush (in a drum-major's way
When the bandsmen march and play).

A yard from the back of the man is the whiteybrown
pony's nose:
He mirrors his master in every item of pace and pose:
He stops when the man stops, without being told,
And seems to be eased by a pause; too plainly he's old,
Indeed, not strength enough shows
To steer the disjointed waggon straight,
Which wriggles left and right in a rambling line,
Deflected thus by its own warp and weight,
And pushing the pony with it in each incline.

The woman walks on the pavement verge,
Parallel to the man:
She wears an apron white and wide in span,
And carries a like Turk's-head, but more in nursing-wise:
Now and then she joins in his dirge,
But as if her thoughts were on distant things.
The rain clams her apron till it clings. –
So, step by step, they move with their merchandize,
And nobody buys.

The Weary Walker

A plain in front of me,
    And there's the road
Upon it. Wide country,
    And, too, the road!

Past the first ridge another,
    And still the road
Creeps on. Perhaps no other
    Ridge for the road?

Ah! Past that ridge a third,
    Which still the road   10
Has to climb furtherward –
    The thin white road!

Sky seems to end its track;
    But no. The road
Trails down the hill at the back.
    Ever the road!

Nobody Comes

Tree-leaves labour up and down,
    And through them the fainting light
    Succumbs to the crawl of night.
Outside in the road the telegraph wire
    To the town from the darkening land
Intones to travellers like a spectral lyre
    Swept by a spectral hand.

A car comes up, with lamps full-glare,
    That flash upon a tree:
    It has nothing to do with me,   10
And whangs along in a world of its own,
    Leaving a blacker air;
And mute by the gate I stand again alone,
    And nobody pulls up there.

9 October 1924

Last Look round St Martin's Fair

The sun is like an open furnace door,
Whose round revealed retort contains the roar
            Of fires beyond terrene;
The moon presents the lustre-lacking face
            Of a brass dial gone green,
            Whose hours no eye can trace.
The unsold heathcroppers are driven home
To the shades of the Great Forest whence they come
By men with long cord-waistcoats in brown monochrome.
10   The stars break out, and flicker in the breeze,
            It seems, that twitches the trees. –
            From its hot idol soon
The fickle unresting earth has turned to a fresh patroon –
            The cold, now brighter, moon.
The woman in red, at the nut-stall with the gun,
            Lights up, and still goes on:
She's redder in the flare-lamp than the sun
            Showed it ere it was gone.
Her hands are black with loading all the day,
20   And yet she treats her labour as 'twere play,
Tosses her ear-rings, and talks ribaldry
To the young men around as natural gaiety,
            And not a weary work she'd readily stay
And never again nut-shooting see,
            Though crying, 'Fire away!'

When Oats Were Reaped

That day when oats were reaped, and wheat was ripe, and
            barley ripening,
            The road-dust hot, and the bleaching grasses dry,
            I walked along and said,
While looking just ahead to where some silent people lie:

'I wounded one who's there, and now know well I wounded
    her;
  But, ah, she does not know that she wounded me!'
    And not an air stirred,
Nor a bill of any bird; and no response accorded she.

August 1913

The Harbour Bridge

From here, the quay, one looks above to mark
The bridge across the harbour, hanging dark
Against the day's-end sky, fair-green in glow
Over and under the middle archway's bow:
It draws its skeleton where the sun has set,
Yea, clear from cutwater to parapet;
On which mild glow, too, lines of rope and spar
  Trace themselves black as char.

Down here in shade we hear the painters shift
Against the bollards with a drowsy lift,   10
As moved by the incoming stealthy tide.
High up across the bridge the burghers glide
As cut black-paper portraits hastening on
In conversation none knows what upon:
Their sharp-edged lips move quickly word by word
  To speech that is not heard.

There trails the dreamful girl, who leans and stops,
There presses the practical woman to the shops,
There is a sailor, meeting his wife with a start,
And we, drawn nearer, judge they are keeping apart. 20
Both pause. She says: 'I've looked for you. I thought
We'd make it up.' Then no words can be caught.
At last: 'Won't you come home?' She moves still nigher:
  ''Tis comfortable, with a fire.'

'No,' he says gloomily. 'And, anyhow,
I can't give up the other woman now:
You should have talked like that in former days,
When I was last home.' They go different ways.
And the west dims, and yellow lamplights shine:
30   And soon above, like lamps more opaline,
White stars ghost forth, that care not for men's wives,
      Or any other lives.

WEYMOUTH

'Not Only I'

Not only I
    Am doomed awhile to lie
In this close bin with earthen sides;
But the things I thought, and the songs I sang,
And the hopes I had, and the passioned pang
    For people I knew
    Who passed before me,
Whose memory barely abides;
    And the visions I drew
10   That daily upbore me!

And the joyous springs and summers,
    And the jaunts with blithe newcomers,
And my plans and appearances; drives and rides
That fanned my face to a lively red;
    And the grays and blues
    Of the far-off views,
That nobody else discerned outspread;
And little achievements for blame or praise;
Things left undone; things left unsaid;
20   In brief, my days!

Compressed here in six feet by two,
     In secrecy
     To lie with me
     Till the Call shall be,
Are all these things I knew,
Which cannot be handed on;
Strange happenings quite unrecorded,
Lost to the world and disregarded,
That only thinks: 'Here moulders till Doom's-dawn
     A woman's skeleton.'   30

Horses Aboard

Horses in horseclothes stand in a row
On board the huge ship, that at last lets go:
Whither are they sailing? They do not know,
Nor what for, nor how. –
     They are horses of war,
And are going to where there is fighting afar;
But they gaze through their eye-holes unwitting they are,
And that in some wilderness, gaunt and ghast,
Their bones will bleach ere a year has passed,
And the item be as 'war-waste' classed. –   10
And when the band booms, and the folk say 'Good-bye!'
And the shore slides astern, they appear wrenched awry
From the scheme Nature planned for them, – wondering
     why.

The Missed Train

     How I was caught
Hieing home, after days of allure,
And forced to an inn – small, obscure –
     At the junction, gloom-fraught.

How civil my face
To get them to chamber me there –
A roof I had scorned, scarce aware
That it stood at the place.

And how all the night
I had dreams of the unwitting cause
Of my lodgment. How lonely I was;
How consoled by her sprite!

Thus onetime to me . . .
Dim wastes of dead years bar away
Then from now. But such happenings to-day
Fall to lovers, may be!

Years, years as shoaled seas,
Truly, stretch now between! Less and less
Shrink the visions then vast in me. – Yes,
Then in me: Now in these.

Cynic's Epitaph

A race with the sun as he downed
I ran at evetide,
Intent who should first gain the ground
And there hide.

He beat me by some minutes then,
But I triumphed anon,
For when he'd to rise up again
I stayed on.

The Sundial on a Wet Day

I drip, drip here
In Atlantic rain,
Falling like handfuls
Of winnowed grain,
Which, tear-like, down
My gnomon drain,
And dim my numerals
With their stain, –
Till I feel useless,
And wrought in vain!   10

And then I think
In my despair
That, though unseen,
He is still up there,
And may gaze out
Anywhen, anywhere;
Not to help clockmen
Quiz and compare,
But in kindness to let me
My trade declare.   20

ST JULIOT

Shortening Days at the Homestead

The first fire since the summer is lit, and is smoking into
        the room:
        The sun-rays thread it through, like woof-lines in a
            loom.
        Sparrows spurt from the hedge, whom misgivings
            appal
That winter did not leave last year for ever, after all.
        Like shock-headed urchins, spiny-haired,
        Stand pollard willows, their twigs just bared.

Who is this coming with pondering pace,
Black and ruddy, with white embossed,
His eyes being black, and ruddy his face,
And the marge of his hair like morning frost?
  It's the cider-maker,
  And appletree-shaker,
And behind him on wheels, in readiness,
His mill, and tubs, and vat, and press.

Days to Recollect

  Do you recall
  That day in Fall
When we walked towards Saint Alban's Head,
Over thistledown that summer had shed,
  Or must I remind you?
Winged thistle-seeds which hitherto
Had lain as none were there, or few,
But rose at the brush of your petticoat-seam
(As ghosts might rise of the recent dead),
And sailed on the breeze in a nebulous stream
  Like a comet's tail behind you:
  You don't recall
  That day in Fall?

  Then do you remember
  That sad November
When you left me never to see me more,
And looked quite other than theretofore,
  As if it could not *be* you?
And lay by the window whence you had gazed
So many times when blamed or praised,
Morning or noon, through years and years,
Accepting the gifts that Fortune bore,
Sharing, enduring, joys, hopes, fears!
  Well: I never more did see you. –
  Say you remember
  That sad November!

The High-School Lawn

Gray prinked with rose,
White tipped with blue,
Shoes with gay hose,
Sleeves of chrome hue;
Fluffed frills of white,
Dark bordered light;
Such shimmerings through
Trees of emerald green are eyed
This afternoon, from the road outside.

They whirl around: 10
Many laughters run
With a cascade's sound;
Then a mere one.
A bell: they flee:
Silence then: –
So it will be
Some day again
With them, – with me.

'Nothing Matters Much'

(B. F. L.)

'Nothing matters much,' he said
Of something just befallen unduly:
He, then active, but now dead,
    Truly, truly!

He knew the letter of the law
As voiced by those of wig and gown,
Whose slightest syllogistic flaw
    He hammered down.

And often would he shape in word
10   That nothing needed much lamenting;
And she who sat there smiled and heard,
    Sadly assenting.

Facing the North Sea now he lies,
Toward the red altar of the East,
The Flamborough roar his psalmodies,
    The wind his priest.

And while I think of his bleak bed,
Of Time that builds, of Time that shatters,
Lost to all thought is he, who said
20   'Nothing much matters.'

'Why Do I?'

Why do I go on doing these things?
    Why not cease?
Is it that you are yet in this world of welterings
    And unease,
And that, while so, mechanic repetitions please?

When shall I leave off doing these things? –
    When I hear
You have dropped your dusty cloak and taken you
    wondrous wings
    To another sphere,
10   Where no pain is: Then shall I hush this dinning gear.

From *Winter Words in Various Moods
and Metres* (1928)

'I Am the One'

I am the one whom ringdoves see
    Through chinks in boughs
    When they do not rouse
    In sudden dread,
But stay on cooing, as if they said:
    'Oh; it's only he.'

I am the passer when up-eared hares,
    Stirred as they eat
    The new-sprung wheat,
    Their munch resume
As if they thought: 'He is one for whom
    Nobody cares.'

Wet-eyed mourners glance at me
    As in train they pass
    Along the grass
    To a hollowed spot,
And think: 'No matter; he quizzes not
    Our misery.'

I hear above: 'We stars must lend
    No fierce regard
    To his gaze, so hard
    Bent on us thus, –
Must scathe him not. He is one with us
    Beginning and end.'

The Mound

For a moment pause: –
Just here it was;
And through the thin thorn hedge, by the rays of the
moon,
I can see the tree in the field, and beside it the mound –
Now sheeted with snow – whereon we sat that June
When it was green and round,
And she crazed my mind by what she coolly told –
The history of her undoing,
(As I saw it), but she called 'comradeship',
That bred in her no rueing:
And saying she'd not be bound
For life to one man, young, ripe-yeared, or old,
Left me – an innocent simpleton to her viewing;
For, though my accompt of years outscored her own,
Hers had more hotly flown . . .
We never met again by this green mound,
To press as once so often lip on lip,
And palter, and pause:–
Yes; here it was!

Evening Shadows

The shadows of my chimneys stretch afar
Across the plot, and on to the privet bower,
And even the shadows of their smokings show,
And nothing says just now that where they are
They will in future stretch at this same hour,
Though in my earthen cyst I shall not know.

And at this time the neighbouring Pagan mound,
Whose myths the Gospel news now supersede,
Upon the greensward also throws its shade,

And nothing says such shade will spread around   10
Even as to-day when men will no more heed
The Gospel news than when the mound was made.

Throwing a Tree

NEW FOREST

The two executioners stalk along over the knolls,
Bearing two axes with heavy heads shining and wide,
And a long limp two-handled saw toothed for cutting
   great boles,
And so they approach the proud tree that bears the death-
   mark on its side.

Jackets doffed they swing axes and chop away just above
   ground,
And the chips fly about and lie white on the moss and
   fallen leaves;
Till a broad deep gash in the bark is hewn all the way
   round,
And one of them tries to hook upward a rope, which at last
   he achieves.

The saw then begins, till the top of the tall giant
   shivers:
The shivers are seen to grow greater each cut than   10
   before:
They edge out the saw, tug the rope; but the tree only
   quivers,
And kneeling and sawing again, they step back to try
   pulling once more.

Then, lastly, the living mast sways, further sways: with
   a shout
Job and Ike rush aside. Reached the end of its long
   staying powers
The tree crashes downward: it shakes all its neighbours
   throughout,
And two hundred years' steady growth has been ended in
   less than two hours.

Lying Awake

You, Morningtide Star, now are steady-eyed, over the east,
    I know it as if I saw you;
You, Beeches, engrave on the sky your thin twigs, even the
        least;
    Had I paper and pencil I'd draw you.

You, Meadow, are white with your counterpane cover of
        dew,
    I see it as if I were there;
You, Churchyard, are lightening faint from the shade of
        the yew,
    The names creeping out everywhere.

He Never Expected Much

[or]
A CONSIDERATION
[A REFLECTION] ON MY EIGHTY-SIXTH BIRTHDAY

Well, World, you have kept faith with me,
    Kept faith with me;
Upon the whole you have proved to be
    Much as you said you were.
Since as a child I used to lie
Upon the leaze and watch the sky,
Never, I own, expected I
    That life would all be fair.

'Twas then you said, and since have said,
    Times since have said,
In that mysterious voice you shed
    From clouds and hills around:
'Many have loved me desperately,
Many with smooth serenity,
While some have shown contempt of me
    Till they dropped underground.

'I do not promise overmuch,
    Child; overmuch;
Just neutral-tinted haps and such,'
    You said to minds like mine.   20
Wise warning for your credit's sake!
Which I for one failed not to take,
And hence could stem such strain and ache
    As each year might assign.

Standing by the Mantelpiece

(H. M. M., 1873)

This candle-wax is shaping to a shroud
To-night. (They call it that, as you may know) –
By touching it the claimant is avowed,
And hence I press it with my finger – so.

To-night. To me twice night, that should have been
The radiance of the midmost tick of noon,
And close around me wintertime is seen
That might have shone the veriest day of June!

But since all's lost, and nothing really lies
Above but shade, and shadier shade below,   10
Let me make clear, before one of us dies,
My mind to yours, just now embittered so.

Since you agreed, unurged and full-advised,
And let warmth grow without discouragement,
Why do you bear you now as if surprised,
When what has come was clearly consequent?

Since you have spoken, and finality
Closes around, and my last movements loom,
I say no more: the rest must wait till we
Are face to face again, yonside the tomb.   20

And let the candle-wax thus mould a shape
Whose meaning now, if hid before, you know,
And how by touch one present claims its drape,
And that it's I who press my finger – so.

Christmas: 1924

'Peace upon earth!' was said. We sing it,
And pay a million priests to bring it.
After two thousand years of mass
We've got as far as poison-gas.

1924

'We Are Getting to the End'

We are getting to the end of visioning
The impossible within this universe,
Such as that better whiles may follow worse,
And that our race may mend by reasoning.

We know that even as larks in cages sing
Unthoughtful of deliverance from the curse
That holds them lifelong in a latticed hearse,
We ply spasmodically our pleasuring.

And that when nations set them to lay waste
Their neighbours' heritage by foot and horse,
And hack their pleasant plains in festering seams,
They may again, – not warely, or from taste,
But tickled mad by some demonic force. –
Yes. We are getting to the end of dreams!

He Resolves to Say No More

O my soul, keep the rest unknown!
It is too like a sound of moan
    When the charnel–eyed
    Pale Horse has nighed:
Yea, none shall gather what I hide!

Why load men's minds with more to bear
That bear already ails to spare?
    From now alway
    Till my last day
What I discern I will not say.   10

Let Time roll backward if it will;
(Magians who drive the midnight quill
    With brain aglow
    Can see it so),
What I have learnt no man shall know.

And if my vision range beyond
The blinkered sight of souls in bond,
    – By truth made free –
    I'll let all be,
And show to no man what I see.   20

Appendix 1:
'Preface' to Select Poems of William Barnes, Chosen and Edited by Thomas Hardy

This volume of verse includes, to the best of my judgement, the greater part of that which is of the highest value in the poetry of William Barnes. I have been moved to undertake the selection by a thought that has overridden some immediate objections to such an attempt, – that I chance to be (I believe) one of the few living persons having a practical acquaintance with letters who knew familiarly the Dorset dialect when it was spoken as Barnes writes it, or, perhaps, who know it as it is spoken now. Since his death, education in the west of England as elsewhere has gone on with its silent and inevitable effacements, reducing the speech of this country to uniformity, and obliterating every year many a fine old local word. The process is always the same: the word is ridiculed by the newly taught; it gets into disgrace; it is heard in holes and corners only; it dies; and, worst of all, it leaves no synonym. In the villages that one recognizes to be the scenes of these pastorals the poet's nouns, adjectives, and idioms daily cease to be understood by the younger generation, the luxury of four demonstrative pronouns, of which he was so proud, vanishes by their compression into the two of common English, and the suffix to verbs which marks continuity of action is almost everywhere shorn away.

To cull from a dead writer's whole achievement in verse portions that shall exhibit him is a task of no small difficulty, and of some temerity. There is involved, first of all, the question of right. A selector may say: These are the pieces that please me best; but he may not be entitled to hold that they are the best in themselves and for everybody. This opens the problem of equating the personality – of adjusting the idiosyncrasy of the chooser to mean pitch. If it can be done in some degree – one may doubt it – there are to be borne in mind the continually changing taste of the times. But, assuming average critical capacity in the compiler, that he represents his own time, and that he finds it no great toil to come to a conclusion on which in his view are the highest levels and the lowest of a poet's execution, the complete field of the work examined almost always contains a large intermediate tract where the accomplishment is of nearly uniform merit throughout, selection from which must be by a process of sampling rather than of gleaning; many a poem, too, of indifferent achievement in its wholeness may contain some line, couplet, or stanza of great excellence; and contrariwise, a bad or irrelevant verse may mar the good remainder; in each case the choice is puzzled, and the balance struck by a single mind can hardly escape being questioned here and there.

A word may be said on the arrangement of the poems as 'lyrical and elegiac'; 'descriptive and meditative'; 'humorous'; a classification which has been adopted with this author in the present volume for the first time. It is an old story that such divisions may be open to grave objection, in respect, at least, of the verse of the majority of poets, who write in the accepted language. For one thing, many fine poems that have lyric moments are not entirely lyrical; many largely narrative poems are not entirely narrative; many personal reflections or meditations in verse hover across the frontiers of lyricism. To this general opinion I would add that the same lines may be lyrical to one temperament and meditative to another; nay, lyrical and not lyrical to the same reader at different times, according to his mood and circumstance. Gray's *Elegy* may be instanced as a poem that has almost made itself notorious by claiming to be a lyric in particular humours, situations, and weathers, and waiving the claim in others.

One might, to be sure, as a smart impromptu, narrow down the definition of lyric to the safe boundary of poetry that has all its nouns in the vocative case, and so settle the question by the simple touchstone of the grammar-book, adducing the *Benedicite* as a shining example. But this qualification would be disconcerting in its stringency, and cause a fluttering of the leaves of many an accepted anthology.

A story which was told the writer by Mr Barnes himself may be apposite here. When a pupil of his was announced in *The Times* as having come out at the top in the Indian Service examination-list of those days, the schoolmaster was overwhelmed with letters from anxious parents requesting him at any price to make their sons come out at the top also. He replied that he willingly would, but that it took two to do it. It depends, in truth, upon the other person, the reader, whether certain numbers shall be raised to lyric pitch or not; and if he does not bring to the page of these potentially lyric productions a lyrical quality of mind, they must be classed, for him, as non-lyrical.

However, to pass the niceties of this question by. In the exceptional instance of a poet like Barnes who writes in a dialect only, a new condition arises to influence considerations of assortment. Lovers of poetry who are but imperfectly acquainted with his vocabulary and idiom may yet be desirous of learning something of his message; and the most elementary guidance is of help to such students, for they are liable to mistake their author on the very threshold. For some reason or none, many persons suppose that when anything is penned in the tongue of the countryside, the primary intent is burlesque or ridicule, and this especially if the speech be one in which the sibilant has the rough sound, and is expressed by Z. Indeed, scores of thriving storytellers and dramatists seem to believe that by transmuting the flattest conversation into a dialect that never existed, and making the talkers say 'be' where they would really say 'is', a Falstaffian richness is at once imparted to its qualities.

But to a person to whom a dialect is native its sounds are as consonant with moods of sorrow as with moods of mirth: there is no grotesqueness in it as such. Nor was there to Barnes. To provide an alien reader with a rough clue to the taste of the kernel that may be expected under the shell of the spelling has seemed to be worth while, and to justify a division into heads that may in some cases appear arbitrary.

In respect of the other helps – the glosses and paraphrases given on each page – it may be assumed that they are but a sorry substitute for the full significance the original words bear to those who read them without translation, and know their delicate ability to express the doings, joys and jests, troubles, sorrows, needs and sicknesses of life in the rural world as elsewhere. The Dorset dialect being – or having been – a tongue, and not a corruption, it is the old question over again, that of the translation of poetry; which, to the full, is admittedly impossible. And further; gesture and facial expression figure so largely in the speech of the husbandmen as to be speech itself; hence in the mind's eye of those who know it in its original setting each word of theirs is accompanied by the qualifying face-play which no construing can express.

It may appear strange to some, as it did to friends in his lifetime, that a man of insight who had the spirit of poesy in him should have persisted year after year in writing in a fast-perishing language, and on themes which in some not remote time would be familiar to nobody, leaving him pathetically like

A ghostly cricket, creaking where a house was burned;

– a language with the added disadvantage by comparison with other dead tongues that no master or books would be readily available for the acquisition of its finer meanings. He himself simply said that he could not help it, no doubt feeling his idylls to be an extemporization, or impulse, without prevision or power of appraisement on his own part.

Yet it seems to the present writer that Barnes, despite this, really belonged to the literary school of such poets as Tennyson, Gray, and Collins, rather than to that of the old unpremeditating singers in dialect. Primarily spontaneous, he was academic closely after; and we find him warbling his native woodnotes with a watchful eye on the predetermined score, a far remove from the popular impression of him as the naif and rude bard who sings only because he must, and who submits the uncouth lines of his page to us without knowing how they come there. Goethe never knew better of his; nor Milton; nor, in their rhymes, Poe; nor, in their whimsical alliterations here and there, Langland and the versifiers of the fourteenth and fifteenth centuries.

In his aim at closeness of phrase to his vision he strained at times the capacities of dialect, and went wilfully outside the dramatization of peasant talk. Such a lover of the art of expression was this penman of a dialect that had no literature, that on some occasions he would allow art to overpower spontaneity and to cripple inspiration; though, be it remembered, he never tampered with the dialect itself. His ingenious internal rhymes, his subtle juxtaposition of kindred lippings and vowel-sounds, show a fastidiousness in word-selection that is surprising in verse which professes to represent the habitual modes of language among the western peasantry. We do not find in the dialect balladists of the seven-teenth century, or in Burns (with whom he has sometimes been measured), such careful finish, such verbal dexterities, such search-ings for the most cunning syllables, such satisfaction with the best phrase. Had he not begun with dialect, and seen himself recog-nized as an adept in it before he had quite found himself as a poet, who knows that he might not have brought upon his muse the disaster that has befallen so many earnest versifiers of recent time, have become a slave to the passion for form, and have wasted all his substance in whittling at its shape.

From such, however, he was saved by the conditions of his scene, characters, and vocabulary. It may have been, indeed, that he saw this tendency in himself, and retained the dialect as a corrective to the tendency. Whether or no, by a felicitous instinct he does at times break into sudden irregularities in the midst of his subtle rhythms and measures, as if feeling rebelled against further drill. Then his self-consciousness ends, and his naturalness is saved.

But criticism is so easy, and art so hard: criticism so flimsy, and the life-seer's voice so lasting. When we consider what such appreciativeness as Arnold's could allow his prejudices to say about the highest-soaring among all our lyricists; what strange criticism Shelley himself could indulge in now and then; that the history of criticism is mainly the history of error, which has not even, as many errors have, quaintness enough to make it interest-ing, we may well doubt the utility of such writing on the sand. What is the use of saying, as has been said of Barnes, that compound epithets like 'the blue-hill'd worold', 'the wide-horn'd cow', 'the grey-topp'd heights of Paladore', are a high-handed enlargement of the ordinary ideas of the field-folk into whose mouths they are put? These things are justified by the art of every age when they can claim to be, as here, singularly precise and beautiful definitions of what is signified; which in these instances, too, apply with double force to the deeply tinged horizon, to the breed of kine, to the aspect of Shaftesbury Hill, characteristic of the Vale within which most of his revelations are enshrined.

Dialect, it may be added, offered another advantage to him as the writer, whatever difficulties it may have for strangers who try to follow it. Even if he often used the dramatic form of peasant speakers as a pretext for the expression of his own mind and experiences – which cannot be doubted – yet he did not always do this, and the assumed character of husbandman or hamleteer enabled him to elude in his verse those dreams and speculations that cannot leave alone the mystery of things, – possibly an unworthy mystery and disappointing if solved, though one that has a harrowing fascination for many poets, – and helped him to fall back on dramatic truth, by making his personages express the notions of life prevalent in their sphere.

As by the screen of dialect, so by the intense localization aforesaid, much is lost to the outsider who by looking into Barnes's pages only revives general recollections of country life. Yet many passages may shine into that reader's mind through the veil which partly hides them; and it is hoped and believed that, even in a superficial reading, something more of this poet's charm will be gathered from the present selection by persons to whom the Wessex R and Z are uncouth misfortunes, and the dying words those of an unlamented language that need leave behind it no grammar of its secrets and no key to its tomb.

T. H.

September 1908

Appendix 2:
'Apology' from Late Lyrics and Earlier

About half the verses that follow were written quite lately. The rest are older, having been held over in MS when past volumes were published, on considering that these would contain a sufficient number of pages to offer readers at one time, more especially during the distractions of the war. The unusually far back poems to be found here are, however, but some that were overlooked in gathering previous collections. A freshness in them, now unattainable, seemed to make up for their inexperience and to justify their inclusion. A few are dated; the dates of others are not discoverable.

The launching of a volume of this kind in neo-Georgian days by one who began writing in mid-Victorian, and has published nothing to speak of for some years, may seem to call for a few words of excuse or explanation. Whether or no, readers may feel assured that a new book is submitted to them with great hesitation at so belated a date. Insistent practical reasons, however, among which were requests from some illustrious men of letters who are in sympathy with my productions, the accident that several of the poems have already seen the light, and that dozens of them have been lying about for years, compelled the course adopted, in spite of the natural disinclination of a writer whose works have been so frequently regarded askance by a pragmatic section here and there, to draw attention to them once more.

I do not know that it is necessary to say much on the contents of the book, even in deference to suggestions that will be mentioned presently. I believe that those readers who care for my poems at all – readers to whom no passport is required – will care for this new instalment of them, perhaps the last, as much as for any that have preceded them. Moreover, in the eyes of a less friendly class the pieces, though a very mixed collection indeed, contain, so far as I am able to see, little or nothing in technic or teaching that can be considered a Star-Chamber matter, or so much as agitating to a ladies' school; even though, to use Words-worth's observation in his Preface to *Lyrical Ballads*, such readers may suppose 'that by the act of writing in verse an author makes a formal engagement that he will gratify certain known habits of association: that he not only thus apprises the reader that certain classes of ideas and expressions will be found in his book, but that others will be carefully excluded'.

It is true, nevertheless, that some grave, positive, stark delinea-tions are interspersed among those of the passive, lighter, and traditional sort presumably nearer to stereotyped tastes. For – while I am quite aware that a thinker is not expected, and, indeed, is scarcely allowed, now more than heretofore, to state all that crosses his mind concerning existence in this universe, in his attempts to explain or excuse the presence of evil and the incongru-ity of penalizing the irresponsible – it must be obvious to open intelligences that, without denying the beauty and faithful service of certain venerable cults, such disallowance of 'obstinate question-ings' and 'blank misgivings' tends to a paralysed intellectual stalemate. Heine observed nearly a hundred years ago that the soul has her eternal rights; that she will not be darkened by statutes, nor lullabied by the music of bells. And what is today, in allusions to the present author's pages, alleged to be 'pessimism' is, in truth, only such 'questionings' in the exploration of reality, and is the first step towards the soul's betterment, and the body's also.

If I may be forgiven for quoting my own old words, let me repeat what I printed in this relation more than twenty years ago, and wrote much earlier, in a poem entitled 'In Tenebris':

> If way to the Better there be, it exacts a full look at the Worst:

that is to say, by the exploration of reality, and its frank recogni-tion stage by stage along the survey, with an eye to the best consummation possible: briefly, evolutionary meliorism. But it is called pessimism nevertheless; under which word, expressed with condemnatory emphasis, it is regarded by many as some pernicious new thing (though so old as to underlie the Gospel scheme, and even to permeate the Greek drama); and the subject is charitably left to decent silence, as if further comment were needless.

Happily there are some who feel such Levitical passing-by to be, alas, by no means a permanent dismissal of the matter; that comment on where the world stands is very much the reverse of needless in these disordered years of our prematurely afflicted century: that amendment and not madness lies that way. And looking down the future these few hold fast to the same: that whether the human and kindred animal races survive till the exhaustion or destruction of the globe, or whether these races perish and are succeeded by others before that conclusion comes, pain to all upon it, tongued or dumb, shall be kept down to a minimum by loving-kindness, operating through scientific knowledge, and actuated by the modicum of free will conjecturally possessed by organic life when the mighty necessitating forces – unconscious or other – that have 'the balancings of the clouds', happen to be in equilibrium, which may or may not be often.

To conclude this question I may add that the argument of the so-called optimists is neatly summarized in a stern pronouncement against me by my friend Mr Frederic Harrison in a late essay of his, in the words: 'This view of life is not mine.' The solemn declaration does not seem to me to be so annihilating to the said 'view' (really a series of fugitive impressions which I have never tried to co-ordinate) as is complacently assumed. Surely it embodies a too human fallacy quite familiar in logic. Next, a knowing reviewer, apparently a Roman Catholic young man, speaks, with some rather gross instances of the *suggestio falsi* in his whole article, of 'Mr Hardy refusing consolation', the 'dark gravity of his ideas', and so on. When a Positivist and a Romanist agree there must be something wonderful in it, which should make a poet sit up. But . . . O that 'twere possible!

I would not have alluded in this place or anywhere else to such casual personal criticisms – for casual and unreflecting they must be – but for the satisfaction of two or three friends in whose opinion a short answer was deemed desirable, on account of the continual repetition of these criticisms, or more precisely, quizzings. After all, the serious and truly literary inquiry in this connection is: Should a shaper of such stuff as dreams are made on disregard considerations of what is customary and expected, and apply himself to the real function of poetry, the application of ideas to life (in Matthew Arnold's familiar phrase)? This bears more particularly on what has been called the 'philosophy' of these poems – usually reproved as 'queer'. Whoever the author may be that undertakes such application of ideas in this 'philosophic' direction – where it is specially required – glacial judgements must inevitably fall upon him amid opinion whose arbiters largely decry individuality, to whom *ideas* are oddities to smile at, who are moved by a yearning the reverse of that of the Athenian inquirers on Mars Hill; and stiffen their features not only at sound of a new thing, but at a restatement of old things in new terms. Hence should anything of this sort in the following adumbrations seem 'queer' – should any of them seem to good Panglossians to embody strange and disrespectful conceptions of this best of all possible worlds, I apologize; but cannot help it.

Such divergences, which, though piquant for the nonce, it would be affectation to say are not saddening and discouraging likewise, may, to be sure, arise sometimes from superficial aspect only, writer and reader seeing the same thing at different angles. But in palpable cases of divergence they arise, as already said, whenever a serious effort is made towards that which the authority I have cited – who would now be called old-fashioned, possibly even parochial – affirmed to be what no good critic could deny as the poet's province, the application of ideas to life. One might shrewdly guess, by the by, that in such recommendation the famous writer may have overlooked the cold-shouldering results upon an enthusiastic disciple that would be pretty certain to follow his putting the high aim in practice, and have forgotten the disconcerting experience of Gil Blas with the Archbishop.

To add a few more words to what has already taken up too many, there is a contingency liable to miscellanies of verse that I have never seen mentioned, so far as I can remember; I mean the chance little shocks that may be caused over a book of various character like the present and its predecessors by the juxtaposition of unrelated, even discordant, effusions; poems perhaps years apart in the making, yet facing each other. An odd result of this has been that dramatic anecdotes of a satirical and humorous intention following verse in graver voice, have been read as misfires because they raise the smile that they were intended to raise, the journalist, deaf to the sudden change of key, being unconscious that he is laughing with the author and not at him. I admit that I did not foresee such contingencies as I ought to have done, and that people might not perceive when the tone altered. But the difficulties of arranging the themes in a graduated kinship of moods would have been so great that irrelation was almost unavoidable with efforts so diverse. I must trust for right note-catching to those finely-touched spirits who can divine without half a whisper, whose intuitiveness is proof against all the accidents of inconsequence. In respect of the less alert, however, should anyone's train of thought be thrown out of gear by a consecutive piping of vocal reeds in jarring tonics, without a semiquaver's rest between, and be led thereby to miss the writer's aim and meaning in one out of two contiguous compositions, I shall deeply regret it.

Having at last, I think, finished with the personal points that I was recommended to notice, I will forsake the immediate object of this Preface; and, leaving *Late Lyrics* to whatever fate it deserves, digress for a few moments to more general considerations. The thoughts of any man of letters concerned to keep poetry alive cannot but run uncomfortably on the precarious prospects of English verse at the present day. Verily the hazards and casualties surrounding the birth and setting forth of almost every modern creation in numbers are ominously like those of one of Shelley's paper-boats on a windy lake. And a forward conjecture scarcely permits the hope of a better time, unless men's tendencies should change. So indeed of all art, literature, and 'high thinking' nowadays. Whether owing to the barbarizing of taste in the younger minds by the dark madness of the late war, the unabashed cultivation of selfishness in all classes, the plethoric growth of knowledge simultaneously with the stunting of wisdom, 'a degrading thirst after outrageous stimulation' (to quote Wordsworth again), or from any other cause, we seem threatened with a new Dark Age.

I formerly thought, like other much exercised writers, that so far as literature was concerned a partial cause might be impotent or mischievous criticism; the satirizing of individuality, the lack of whole-seeing in contemporary estimates of poetry and kindred work, the knowingness affected by junior reviewers, the overgrowth of meticulousness in their peerings for an opinion, as if it were a cultivated habit in them to scrutinize the toolmarks and be blind to the building, to hearken for the key-creaks and be deaf to the diapason, to judge the landscape by a nocturnal exploration with a flash-lantern. In other words, to carry on the old game of sampling the poem or drama by quoting the worst line or worst passage only, in ignorance or not of Coleridge's proof that a versification of any length neither can be nor ought to be all poetry; of reading meanings into a book that its author never dreamt of writing there. I might go on interminably.

But I do not now think any such temporary obstructions to be the cause of the hazard, for these negligences and ignorances, though they may have stifled a few true poets in the run of generations, disperse like stricken leaves before the wind of next week, and are no more heard of again in the region of letters than their writers themselves. No: we may be convinced that something of the deeper sort mentioned must be the cause.

In any event poetry, pure literature in general, religion – I include religion, in its essential and undogmatic sense, because poetry and religion touch each other, or rather modulate into each other; are, indeed, often but different names for the same thing – these, I say, the visible signs of mental and emotional life, must like all other things keep moving, becoming; even though at present, when belief in witches of Endor is displacing the Darwinian theory and 'the truth that shall make you free', men's minds appear, as above noted, to be moving backwards rather than on. I speak somewhat sweepingly, and should except many thoughtful writers in verse and prose; also men in certain worthy but small bodies of various denominations, and perhaps in the homely quarter where advance might have been the very least expected a few years back – the English Church – if one reads it rightly as showing evidence of 'removing those things that are shaken', in accordance with the wise Epistolary recommendation to the Hebrews. For since the historic and once august hierarchy of Rome some generation ago lost its chance of being the religion of the future by doing otherwise, and throwing over the little band of New Catholics who were making a struggle for continuity by applying the principle of evolution to their own faith, joining hands with modern science, and outflanking the hesitating English instinct towards liturgical restatement (a flank march which I at the time quite expected to witness, with the gathering of many millions of waiting agnostics into its fold); since then, one may ask, what other purely English establishment than the Church, of sufficient dignity and footing, with such strength of old association, such scope for transmutability, such architectural spell, is left in this country to keep the shreds of morality together?*

It may indeed be a forlorn hope, a mere dream, that of an alliance between religion, which must be retained unless the world is to perish, and complete rationality, which must come, unless also the world is to perish, by means of the interfusing effect of poetry – 'the breath and finer spirit of all knowledge; the impassioned expression of science', as it was defined by an English poet who was quite orthodox in his ideas. But if it be true, as Comte argued, that advance is never in a straight line, but in a looped orbit, we may, in the aforesaid ominous moving backward, be doing it *pour mieux sauter*, drawing back for a spring. I repeat that I forlornly hope so, notwithstanding the supercilious regard of hope by Schopenhauer, von Hartmann, and other philosophers down to Einstein who have my respect. But one dares not prophesy. Physical, chronological, and other contingencies keep me in these days from critical studies and literary circles

> Where once we held debate, a band
> Of youthful friends, on mind and art

(if one may quote Tennyson in this century). Hence I cannot know how things are going so well as I used to know them, and the aforesaid limitations must quite prevent my knowing henceforward.

I have to thank the editors and owners of *The Times*, *Fortnightly*,

---

* However, one must not be too sanguine in reading signs, and since the above was written evidence that the Church will go far in the removal of 'things that are shaken' has not been encouraging.

Mercury, and other periodicals in which a few of the poems have appeared for kindly assenting to their being reclaimed for collected publication.

T. H.

February 1922

Notes

The following abbreviations are used in the notes:

Hardy's Works

CP, 1919	*Collected Poems*, 1919
CP, 1923	*Collected Poems*, 1923
CP, 1928	*Collected Poems*, 1928
Letters	*Collected Letters of Thomas Hardy*, ed. Richard Little Purdy and Michael Millgate, 1978–88, vols. I–VII
Life	Florence Emily Hardy, *The Life of Thomas Hardy: 1840–1928*, 1962. For convenience I cite this one-volume publication of *The Early Life of Thomas Hardy: 1840–1891* and *The Later Years of Thomas Hardy: 1892–1928*, and treat it, except for the last chapter, as Thomas Hardy's work.
MV	*Moments of Vision and Miscellaneous Verses*, 1917
PPP	*Poems of the Past and the Present*, 1901
SC	*Satires of Circumstance, Lyrics and Reveries*, 1914
SP	*Selected Poems*, 1916
TL	*Time's Laughingstocks and Other Verses*, 1909
WP	*Wessex Poems and Other Verses*, 1898
Works	*The Complete Poetical Works of Thomas Hardy*, ed. Samuel Hynes, 1982–5, vols. I–III

Other

Bailey	J. O. Bailey, *The Poetry of Thomas Hardy*, 1970
Davie	Donald Davie, *Thomas Hardy and British Poetry*, 1972
Deacon/Coleman	Lois Deacon and Terry Coleman, *Providence and Mr Hardy*, 1966
Gittings I	Robert Gittings, *Young Thomas Hardy*, 1975
Gittings II	Robert Gittings, *The Older Hardy*, 1978
Gunn	Thom Gunn, 'Hardy and the Ballads', in *The Occasions of Poetry*, 1982
Hynes	Samuel Hynes, *The Pattern of Hardy's Poetry*, 1961
Millgate	Michael Millgate, *Thomas Hardy: A Biography*, 1982
Paulin	Tom Paulin, *Thomas Hardy: The Poetry of Perception*, 1975
Ransom	John Crowe Ransom, 'Old Age of an Eagle', in *Poems and Essays*, 1955

Domicilium

Published in a pamphlet printed by Clement Shorter (1916); then in *The Early Life of Thomas Hardy* (1928), where Hardy introduces the poem by noting that it was 'written between 1857 and 1860', and remarking: 'Some Wordsworthian lines – the earliest discoverable of Hardy's attempts in verse – give with obvious and naïve fidelity the appearance of the paternal homestead at a date nearly half a century after his great-grandfather had built for their residence the first house in the valley' (*Life*, p. 4). Hardy's great-grandfather, John Hardy, built the homestead in 1800 for his son, Thomas Hardy, who had recently married Mary Head. The poem draws on Hardy's memories of Mary Head, who lived in her son's house from around the time of her grandson's birth, and presumably was occasioned by her death in 1857.

With the exception of many un-Wordsworthian speeches in *The Dynasts* and the rhythmically irregular, Browningesque 'The Collector Cleans His Picture' (*CP*, 1928, pp. 584–5), 'Domicilium' is Hardy's only poem in blank verse.

From *Wessex Poems and Other Verses* (1898)

Neutral Tones

Published 1898; but, as Hardy's date after the poem indicates, written in 1867. *SP* adds the note 'Westbourne Park Villas', where Hardy rented a flat from some time in 1866 until July 1867 (*Gittings I*, p. 238), and where he experienced his first great outpouring of poems.

Exactly when Hardy wrote the poem has been the subject of some unnecessary conjecture. Lois Deacon and Terry Coleman, in an effort to connect the poem with the affair they believe Hardy had with his cousin Tryphena Sparks, suggest that though the poem 'is dated at the foot, "1867" . . . perhaps this indicates not the year in which it was composed but the year in which Hardy and Tryphena became lovers, a year of hopefulness at first, but one which led to the despair of 1871' (*Deacon/Coleman*, p. 82). J. O. Bailey thinks that 'Such evasive dating, perhaps to conceal the fact, is a possibility' (*Bailey*, p. 56). But Hardy's foot-dates in *WP* all refer to times of composition, a fact he makes plain enough in the last paragraph of the book's preface: 'The dates attached to some of the poems do not apply to the rough sketches given in illustration [the first edition of *WP* included drawings by Hardy], which have been recently made . . .'

The identity of Hardy's lover is a mystery. Michael Millgate believes she is Eliza Nichols, to whom Hardy was engaged from 1863 to 1867, but who broke off with him because of his 'infatuation' with her sister Jane Nichols (*Millgate*, p. 100). Robert Gittings thinks 'It is just possible' that the poem concerns a girl in London whom Hardy mentions in a letter only as 'H. A.' (*Gittings I*, p. 93).

Critics have also disagreed about the poem's style. Samuel Hynes sees 'the plain but not quite colloquial language, the hard, particular, colourless images, the slightly odd stanza-form, the dramatic handling of the occasion, the refusal to resolve the issue' as being traits of 'Hardy's most characteristic style', and asserts that 'the style of "Neutral Tones" is essentially that of "The Voice"', a poem written forty-five years later (*Hynes*, pp. 136, 139). More perceptively, John Lucas remarks that as you read the poems of Hardy's maturity, of which 'The Voice' and 'The Shadow on the Stone' are two very great examples, 'you are aware of the absolute transparency of the medium that Hardy uses, and in this they are very unlike his great poem of failed vision, "Neutral Tones", with its self-conscious, deadly awareness of a world blighted by the failure of a love-relationship', and its 'appalling, flat rhythms' ('Thomas Hardy: Voices and Visions', in *Modern English Poetry from Hardy to Hughes*, 1986, p. 35). I should dissent from 'appalling', rather noting some unsuccessful moments in the poem that seem to me characteristic of Hardy's early idiom: the easy rhetoric of 'wrings with wrong'; the expository murkiness of l. 8, the original version of which, 'On which was more wrecked by our love' (*Works*, I, p. 13), was only just murkier; and the slightly inexact usage, for the sake of the rhyme, of 'thereby' in l. 11.

John Crowe Ransom (*Ransom*, pp. 80–82) is brilliant in identifying the poem's stanza as one of Hardy's many

variations upon the 'folk line', which nowadays we call dipodic line ... There are just two things to look for if we would hear the dipodic rhythm. The lines are symmetrical, or balanced in the middle, and so are their fractions. The original folk-line had eight beats with a break in the middle; but by division arose the four-beater, with its own break in the middle ... hence the term dipodic, meaning that the line has two beats at least, and if longer has a number of beats which is some power of two. The other feature is perhaps the crucial one. Often a four-beat or eight-beat line will drop its last beat and look unbalanced; but so strong is the dipodic expectation that we allow for the missing beat by a full musical pause. Thus the folk rhythm has an extra musical quality, not in the syllabic or university poetry at all. It is tuneful ... Yet the poet is sufficiently versed in the university meters to know that not only must there not be more than two unstressed syllables between the beat-syllables, but that *fallen* may count as a single syllable, according to a usage established by the stately poets of the Renaissance. He is at pains also to put the comma exactly in the musical middle of the fourth line after *ash*, as if to oblige us to make the one-beat pause at the end.

Among the numerous other discussions of the poem, perhaps Hardy's most known, see especially Stephen Tapscott, 'The Poem Of Trauma', *American Poetry Review*, November/December 1984, pp. 39–41.

Friends Beyond

Published 1898. Hardy drew some of the poem's characters from life; most appear in his Wessex novels. See *Bailey*, pp. 92–5, for a full account.

Again, John Crowe Ransom is illuminating on the poem's prosody (*Ransom*, p. 83):

The stanza here is composed of two rhymed eight-beaters holding suspended between them a four-beater which is unrhymed. But its attachment looks forward: In the following stanza it will give its rhyme to the two eight-beaters; and there a new four-beater will arise to give rhyme to the next stanza, and so on by unbroken progression through the twelve stanzas of the poem. This rhyme-scheme is no more nor less than that of Dante's *terza rima*, a form exalted among university poets. We have attended a startling marriage between the high and the low.

Thoughts of Phena

Published 1898 as 'Thoughts of Ph—a'; then in *SP* as 'At News of a Woman's Death'. Hardy mentions the poem in a journal entry dated 5 March 1890 but obviously written later: '. . . In a train on the way to London. Wrote the first four or six lines of "Not a line of her writing have I". It was a curious instance of sympathetic telepathy. The woman whom I was thinking of – a cousin – was dying at the time, and I quite in ignorance of it. She died six days later. The remainder of the piece was not written till after her death' (*Life*, p. 224). On the scholarly controversy concerning Hardy and Tryphena Sparks, see the notes to 'Neutral Tones' (p. 208) and 'The Recalcitrants' (p. 224).

In a Wood

Published 1898; but it 'was begun in 1887 and completed in 1896' (*Bailey*, p. 97). The poem resembles a passage in chapter VII of Hardy's novel *The Woodlanders* (1887), but does not appear in it.

SP omits the note after the title.

'I Look Into My Glass'

Published 1898. On 18 October 1892 Hardy wrote in his journal (*Life*, p. 251): 'Hurt my tooth at breakfast-time. I look in the glass. Am conscious of the humiliating sorriness of my earthly tabernacle, and of the sad fact that the best of parents could do no better for me . . . Why should a man's mind have been thrown into such close, sad, sensational, inexplicable relations with such a precarious object as his own body!' The poem resembles a passage in Part II, chapter XII of Hardy's novel *The Well-Beloved*, which ran serially in the *Illustrated London News* (October–December 1892): 'When was it to end – this curse of his heart not ageing while his frame moved naturally onward?'

Line 6 reads in a printer's copy 'By friendships lost to me' (*Works*, I, p. 106), but whether the source of the poem's complaint is Hardy's estrangement from Emma or from other 'hearts' is a matter of speculation.

From *Poems of the Past and the Present* (1901)

Drummer Hodge

First published in *Literature*, 25 November 1899, as 'The Dead Drummer', with the note: 'One of the Drummers killed was a native of a village near Casterbridge.' This may be an assertion of imaginative fact: the name Hodge was city-slang for a country boy. Robert Gittings (*Gittings I*, p. 141) notes the influence of Housman's *A Shropshire Lad* (1896).

A Wife in London

Published 1901, with the two parts subtitled 'The Tragedy' and 'The Irony'. Samuel Hynes's observation (*Hynes*, p. 44) that Hardy 'dropped the subtitles from the version of the poem included in *Collected Poems* – persuaded, apparently, that the irony was self-evident' is surely correct. The poem 'was first written, as the manuscript shows, in the first person, with the woman speaking' (*Gittings II*, p. 140).

The Souls of the Slain

First published in the *Cornhill Magazine*, April 1900, with the headnote: 'The spot indicated in the following poem is the Bill of Portland, which stands, roughly, on a line drawn from South Africa to the middle of the United Kingdom; in other words, the flight of a bird along a "great circle" of the earth, cutting through South Africa and the British Isles, might land him at Portland Bill. The "Race" is the turbulent sea-area off the Bill, where contrary tides meet. "Spawls" are the chips of freestone left by the quarriers.'

In Hardy's 'moving commitment to ordinary, unheroic, human values', expressed as a 'wish to commemorate the soldiers who were killed in a foreign land ... by imagining them returning to their native coasts as ghostly birds', Tom Paulin detects a debt to Venulus' speech against war in *Aeneid*, XI (*Paulin*, pp. 49–50). For a discussion of Swinburnian traces in the poem, see *Gittings I*, pp. 141–2.

Shelley's Skylark

Published 1901; the second of eleven 'Poems of Pilgrimage'. Hardy and Emma toured Italy in the spring of 1887, but saw Leghorn, where Shelley composed his ode, 'only from the train window' (*Millgate*, p. 281). Presumably Hardy wrote the poem in 1899 or 1900 from mental or journal notes made fourteen years before. Like Swinburne, Hopkins, Bridges and several other Victorian poets, Hardy thought Shelley 'the highest-soaring among all our lyricists' ('Preface', *Selected Poems of William Barnes*, ed. Thomas Hardy, 1908, p. x). Line 24 originally began 'Heights unsurpassed' (*Works*, I, p. 133).

Rome: At the Pyramid of Cestius near the Graves of Shelley and Keats

Published 1901; the seventh of the 'Poems of Pilgrimage'. Hardy visited the graves in April 1887, but the poem 'was probably not written till later ...' (*Life*, p. 189). The source of l. 14 is Acts 9:1: 'And Saul, yet breathing out threatenings and slaughter against the disciples of the Lord, went unto the high priest.'

The Subalterns

First published in *Academy*, 23 November 1901. John Crowe Ransom comments: 'The measure here is C. M. or Common Measure; Hardy would have known it very well from the many hymns he had sung as a youth. Their tunes lingered nostalgically in his mind even after he had lost his faith ...' ('Introduction', *Selected Poems of Thomas Hardy*, 1960, p. xiv).

In the phrase 'ere when' (l. 19), the second word is fill-in to make the rhyme. Hardy's use of the poetic 'ere' is inconsistent and on several occasions just expedient. In the last two lines of 'In Time of "The Breaking of Nations"' – '"War's annals will cloud into night/Ere their story die" – he treats it as an Old English conjunction requiring the subjunctive 'die'; but in the first stanza of 'Drawing Details in an Old Church', where the word doesn't affect the rhyme – 'And I catch the toll that follows/From the lagging bell,/Ere it spreads to hills and hollows' – he uses it as a modern conjunction taking the indicative 'spreads'.

To Lizbie Browne

Published 1901. In the *Life* (pp. 25–6), Hardy remembers her as 'another young girl, a gamekeeper's pretty daughter, who won Hardy's boyish admiration because of her beautiful bay-red hair. But she despised him, as being two or three years her junior, and married early.' The girl's name was really Elizabeth Bishop (*Millgate*, p. 57).

A Broken Appointment

Published 1901. Michael Millgate believes the poem meditates on Hardy's 'relationship' with Mrs Florence Henniker, whom Hardy met and, to some degree, fell for in May 1893, and that 'it implicitly brings against Mrs Henniker a charge of hardness, of selfishness . . . and she does indeed seem – for all her charm and her passionate advocacy of humanitarian causes – to have been a little lacking in personal warmth: Florence Hardy, who was very fond of her, once said of Sir George Douglas that he appreciated Mrs Henniker, "as few did"' (*Millgate*, p. 341).

Several critics have extolled the poem's moral dignity (see especially J. Middleton Murry, *Aspects of Literature*, 1920, pp. 130–31; *Hynes*, pp. 58–60; and Irving Howe, *Thomas Hardy*, 1967, p. 165). *Paulin* (p. 77) supplies the corrective: 'The poem dramatizes an emotion which is unashamedly passive and self-pitying, its argument is a piece of emotional blackmail in which the man pleads for the woman's pity because he knows he can't have her love. And yet one can't help being impressed by its sheer power and brilliance.'

Birds at Winter Nightfall

Published 1901. Written December 1899 (*Bailey*, p. 163). Along with the villanelle, the sestina and the rondeau, the triolet is one of the medieval French forms that poets of Hardy's generation – Swinburne, Bridges, Dobson, Gosse, Andrew Lang, Stevenson and W. E. Henley – experimented with in the 1870s and 1880s. Hardy would have been familiar with the forms not only from the work of these poets, but from Gosse's manifesto 'A Plea for Certain Exotic Forms of Verse', which appeared in the *Cornhill Magazine* in July 1877, and from *Ballades and Rondeaus* (1887), a retrospective anthology edited by Gleeson White, a copy of which Florence Henniker gave Hardy in the early 1890s (*Letters*, II, p. 24). For an excellent history of the recovery of these forms by Victor Hugo, Sainte-Beuve and Théodore de Banville, and of the influence of these poets on later Victorian poets, see Helen Louise Cohen, *Lyric Forms from France* (1922).

Cohen writes of the triolet: 'The early eight-line form of the rondeau was later given the name of triolet, possibly because, in the first place, it was originally a three-part song. It was only in the fifteenth century, after the creation of the two variant types, that the eight-line poem became known as the triolet.' In her section on the rondeau, Cohen offers the following poem, by the thirteenth-century poet Guillaume d'Amiens, as an example of 'the earliest type of stanza built up in the course of choral song':

> Hareu! commant m'i maintendrai
> Qu'Amors ne m'i laissent durer?
>
> Apansez sui que j'en ferai;
> *Hareu! commant m'i maintendrai?*

A ma dame consoil prendrai
Que bien me le savra doner.
Hareu! commant m'i maintendrai
Qu'Amors ne m'i laissent durer?

'Birds at Winter Nightfall' is one of seven triolets in *PPP*.

The Darkling Thrush

First published as 'By the Century's Deathbed' in the *Graphic*, 29 December 1900. If one includes 'The Last Chrysanthemum' ('Why should this flower delay so long/To show its tremulous plumes?/Now is the time of plaintive robin-song . . .'), the poem is the last of six consecutive bird-poems in *PPP*. John Berryman, in an otherwise confused essay ('Hardy and His Thrush', in *The Freedom of the Poet*, 1976, pp. 242–4), links the poem with the first in the series, 'The Caged Thrush Freed and Home Again', commenting that the subject of its first line, 'Men know but little more than we', 'is an inversion of the "The Darkling Thrush" theme, where the birds know more'. That this is the theme of 'The Darkling Thrush', and that the bird is a poet-figure whose joyous singing expresses Hardy's 'tentative belief in progress' (*Paulin*, p. 152) at the beginning of a new century, is the critical consensus. But the third stanza states plainly that the 'aged thrush' chooses to 'fling his soul/Upon the growing gloom' out of something like avian spite, as if he were determined to pit his passion against the desolation of the landscape; and the final stanza states with equal clarity that it is precisely because the poet sees 'So little cause for carolings', so little reason to hope for anything better from the new century, that he can think the bird knows of 'Some blessed Hope'. This is irony mounting into noble perversity.

The Ruined Maid

Published 1901. Praising the 'ferocity of the young poet of 1866', John Crowe Ransom observed that the poem 'is easier for the gentle reader to take now than it would have been about a century ago' (*Ransom*, pp. 84–5).

The Self-Unseeing

Published 1901. In the *Life* (p. 15), Hardy recollects that as a small boy

He was of ecstatic temperament, extraordinarily sensitive to music, and among the endless jigs, hornpipes, reels, waltzes, and country-dances that his father played of an evening in his early married years, and to which the boy danced a *pas seul* in the middle of the room, there were three or four that always moved the child to tears, though he strenuously tried to hide them.

In Tenebris I

Published 1901 as 'De Profundis'. Epigraph: Psalm 102:4, 'My heart is smitten, and withered like grass' (Authorized Version).

In Tenebris II

Published 1901 as 'De Profundis'. Epigraph: Psalm 142:4, 'I looked on my right hand, and beheld, but there was no man that would know me . . . no man cared for my soul' (Authorized Version).

Sapphic Fragment

Published 1901. Epigraph i: Edward Fitzgerald, *The Rubáiyát of Omar Khayyám*, stanza XLVII. Epigraph ii: *Henry V*, I.ii.229. The poem is a translation of a four-line fragment. Hardy wrote to Swinburne on 1 April 1897 (*Letters*, II, p. 158):

. . . one day, when examining several English imitations of a well-known fragment of Sappho, I interested myself in trying to strike out a better equivalent for it than the commonplace 'Thou, too, shalt die' &c. which all the translators had used during the last hundred years. I then stumbled upon your 'Thee, too, the years shall cover', & all my spirit for poetic pains died out of me. Those few words present, I think, the finest *drama* of Death & Oblivion, so to speak, in our tongue. Having rediscovered this phrase, it carried me back to the buoyant time of 30 years ago, when I used to read your early works walking along the crowded London streets, to my imminent risk of being knocked down.

From Victor Hugo

Published 1901. The poem is a translation of 'À une femme':

> Enfant! si j'étais roi, je donnerais l'empire,
> Et mon char, et mon sceptre, et mon peuple à genoux,
> Et ma couronne d'ore, et mes bains de porphyre,
> Et mes flottes, à qui la mer ne peut suffire,
>   Pour un regard de vous!
>
> Si j'étais Dieu, la terre et l'air avec les ondes,
> Les anges, les démons courbés devant ma loi,
> Et le profond chaos aux entrailles fécondes,
> L'éternité, l'espace, et les cieux, et les mondes,
>   Pour un baiser de toi!

From *Time's Laughingstocks and Other Verses* (1909)

A Trampwoman's Tragedy

First published in *North American Review*, November 1903, with the headnote 'The incidents on which this tale is based occurred in 1827'. Why the poem first appeared there and not in an English magazine Hardy explains in the *Life* (pp. 317–18): 'When the ballad was read in England by the few good judges who met with it, they reproached Hardy with sending it out of the country for publication, not knowing that it was first offered to the *Cornhill Magazine*, and declined by the editor on the ground of it not being a poem he could possibly print in a family periodical.' A few pages earlier (pp. 311–12), Hardy remarks that he 'considered this, upon the whole, his most successful poem', though in a letter of September 1910 to Sir Frederick Macmillan, his publisher, he expressed a more modest and mercantile view of it: 'Tragic narrative poems, like the Trampwoman's Tragedy, seem to be liked most, & I can do them with ease' (*Letters*, IV, p. 117).

A Sunday Morning Tragedy

First published in the *English Review*, December 1908. Hardy first sent the poem to the *Fortnightly Review*, but, as he explained in a letter to Ford Madox Ford (then Hueffer), 'The Editor . . . said that he would have personally liked to print it, but that his review circulated amongst young people.' Hardy goes on with unusual insistence: 'Of course, with a larger morality, the guardians of young people would see that it is the very thing they ought to read, for nobody can say that the treatment is other than moral, & the crime is one of growing prevalence, as you probably know, & the false shame which leads to it is produced by the hypocrisy of the age' (*Letters*, III, p. 331). Ford ('Thomas Hardy', in *Portraits from Life*, 1920, pp. 91–106) later claimed, with an elaborate, self-endorsing hold on fact, to have established the *English Review* in order to publish Hardy's poem. Robert Gittings reveals that Hardy was so taken with the subject of the poem that he 'even planned to make a short play of it, called *Birthwort*, since it hinged on a herbal abortifacient, provided by a "subtle man"' (*Gittings II*, p. 184).

The House of Hospitalities

First published in the *New Quarterly*, January 1909.

Bereft

Published 1909. Few critics have mentioned this poem, but I agree with Samuel Hynes that it is 'one of Hardy's finest poems' (*Hynes*, p. 70). The refrain recalls the final stanza of the ballad, *Barbara Allan*:

> 'O mother, mother, make my bed,
>   O make it saft and narrow,
> Since my love died for me today,
>   I'll die for him tomorrow.'

Autumn in King's Hintock Park

First published in the *Daily Mail Books Supplement*, 17 November 1906, as 'Autumn in my Lord's Park'; then in *TL* as 'Autumn in the Park'. Written in 1901. Hardy wrote to Mrs Henniker: 'How *could* you guess that those lines of mine in the Daily Mail referred to the Ilchesters' park? I happened to be walking, or cycling, through it years ago, when the incident occurred on which the verses are based, & I wrote them out, though I had no intention of publishing them in a newspaper' (*Letters*, III, p. 242). But Robert Gittings claims that Hardy's maternal grandmother 'is almost certainly the subject of the poem' (*Gittings II*, pp. 148–9). See the *Life* (p. 6) for Hardy's contention that his family on his mother's side once owned a house on land that later became part of King's Hintock Park.

Shut Out That Moon

Published 1909.

Reminiscences of a Dancing Man

First published in *Collier's*, 27 March 1909. Several times in his autobiography Hardy recalls nostalgically the dances he attended while living as a young architect in London; for instance (*Life*, pp. 42–3):

Balls were constant at Willis's Rooms, earlier Almack's, and in 1862 Hardy danced at these rooms . . . He used to recount that in those old days, the pretty Lancers and Caledonians were still footed there to the original charming tunes, which brought out the beauty of the figures as no later tunes did, and every movement was a correct quadrille step and gesture. For those dances had not at that date degenerated to a waltzing step, to be followed by galloping romps to uproarious pieces.

Hardy's rectitude here is undercut by Robert Gittings's discovery that 'the girls' at Almack's and Willis's 'were all prostitutes, and their clients moneyed men of pleasure, prepared to spend, in modern terms, at least fifty pounds a night' (*Gittings II*, pp. 58–9). Or did Hardy, who was in his early twenties when he attended the 'Balls', not know?

On the Departure Platform

Published 1909. The poem has to do with Florence Dugdale, who became, in 1914, Hardy's second wife. At the time that Hardy wrote it, he and Miss Dugdale were discreetly seeing one another, usually in London, and even made short trips together by train. His marriage to Emma is the answer to the question in the last stanza.

'I Say I'll Seek Her'

Published 1909. 'Hindrance' (l. 2) is 'peril' in *TL*.

The Night of the Dance

Published 1909.

The Ballad-Singer

First published in the *Cornhill Magazine*, April 1902. This poem and the two that follow here appeared in *TL* under the section title 'A Set of Country Songs' and the group title 'At Casterbridge Fair'.

Former Beauties

Published 1909.

The Inquiry

Published 1909.

A Church Romance

First published in the *Saturday Review*, 8 September 1906; but, according to Hardy (*Letters*, III, p. 226), written 'some time' (I take him to mean 'much') earlier. Hardy quotes the poem in the *Life* (p. 13) after giving this description of his parents' first meeting:

Mrs Hardy [Hardy's mother] once described him [Hardy's father] to her son as he was when she first set eyes on him in the now removed west gallery of Stinsford Church, appearing to her more travelled glance (she had lived for a time in London, Weymouth, and other towns) and somewhat satirical vision, 'rather amusingly old-fashioned, in spite of being decidedly good-looking – wearing the blue swallow-tailed coat with gilt embossed buttons then customary, a red and black flowered waistcoat, Wellington boots, and French-blue trousers.'

The Christening

Published 1909.

After the Last Breath

Published 1909, without the headnote. In the *Life* (p. 321) Hardy eulogizes his mother.

She was now in her ninety-first year, and though she had long suffered from deafness was mentally as clear and alert as ever. She sank gradually, but it was not till two days before her death that she failed to comprehend his words to her. She died on Easter Sunday, April 3, and was buried at Stinsford in the grave of her husband. She had been a woman with an extraordinary store of local memories, reaching back to the days when the ancient ballads were everywhere heard at country feasts, in weaving shops, and at spinning-wheels; and her good taste in literature was expressed by the books she selected for her children in circumstances in which opportunities for selection were not numerous. The portraits of her which appeared in the *Sphere*, the *Gentlewoman*, the *Book Monthly*, and other papers – the best being from a painting by her daughter Mary – show a face of dignity and judgement.

Hardy appears to have loved, admired and honoured his mother unstintingly, and was the first to admit that she had exerted the profoundest influence on his life.

The Pine Planters

Part I published 1909; part II first published in the *Cornhill Magazine*, June 1903, with this headnote: 'The man fills in the earth; the sad-faced woman holds the tree upright, and meditates.' Marty South is a character in Hardy's novel *The Woodlanders* (see chapter VIII for the corresponding passage).

The Man He Killed

First published in *Harper's Weekly* (New York), 8 November 1902; then in England in the *Sphere*, 22 November 1902. In both there appeared the headnote: 'Scene: *The settle of the Fox Inn, Stagfoot Lane.* Characters: *The speaker (a returned soldier), and his friends, natives of the hamlet.*'
    A 'nipperkin' (l. 4) is a measure or vessel for liquors, holding half a pint.

From *Satires of Circumstance, Lyrics and Reveries* (1914)

Channel Firing

First published in the *Fortnightly Review*, 1 May 1914. Hardy (*Life*, p. 365) came to think that the poem had been 'prophetic' of the 'Red war' that began four months after its publication. J. O. Bailey notes that '"Stourton Tower" is the

Alfred Tower about three miles north of Stourton and a little more than thirty miles north of Portland Harbour on the Channel. It is a triangular brick monument about 160 feet high, erected in 1766 to commemorate the victory of Alfred the Great over the invading Danes in a battle near this spot in the year 879' (*Bailey*, p. 263). The name 'Stourton' derives from the Teutonic 'sturmoz', and meant in Middle English an armed conflict.

The Convergence of the Twain

First published in the programme of the 'Dramatic and Operatic Matinée in Aid of the "Titanic" Disaster Fund' held at Covent Garden on 14 May 1912, with the headnote '*Improvised on the loss of "The Titanic"*'; then in the *Fortnightly Review*, 1 June 1912. Written on 24 April 1912 (*Gittings II*, p. 199). Hardy appears to have felt no hesitation in contributing the poem, whose theme is man's ignorant 'Pride' in his technological prowess, to help raise funds for survivors of the *Titanic*. Hardy's attitude in the poem (one shared by Conrad and other contemporary commentators on the disaster) seems all the more severely professional in light of '*Improvised*' in the headnote and his having known two of the drowned passengers (*Letters*, IV, p. 211). Among the several excellent discussions of the poem, see especially *Davie* (p. 11), where one of Hardy's better critics argues that the poem does not present 'a condemnation of technological presumption', but 'very markedly censures the vanity and luxury which created and inhabited the staterooms of the ocean liner'; and Joseph Brodsky, 'The poet, the loved one and the Muse' (*Times Literary Supplement*, 26 October–1 November 1990, pp. 1150, 1160), who sees in the poem's marriage trope a connection with Hardy's elegies for his first wife, 'Poems of 1912–13'.

After the Visit

First published in the *Spectator*, 13 August 1910, without the headnote. Hardy married Florence Emily Dugdale in 1914, thus making the 'strange laws' (l. 23) against divorce no longer an issue for them.

'When I Set Out for Lyonnesse'

Published 1914. The poem recalls Hardy's trip to Cornwall ('Lyonnesse') in March of 1870 when he met Emma for the first time. Hardy liked the poem for its fidelity to experience – 'It is exactly what happened 44 years ago' (*Letters*, V, p. 70) – always for him a high poetic virtue. Happy to hear that the poem was popular in the United States, he praised it for possessing 'the song-ecstasy that a lyric should have (other than an elegiac lyric)' (*ibid.*, p. 199).

A Thunderstorm in Town

Published 1914. 'She' is Mrs Henniker.

'My Spirit Will Not Haunt the Mound'

First published in *Poetry and Drama*, December 1913.

Wessex Heights

Published 1914; but written in December 1896 (*Gittings II*, p. 123). In December 1914 Florence Hardy wrote to a friend (*ibid.*, p. 124):

When I read 'Wessex Heights' it wrung my heart. It made me miserable to think that he had ever suffered so much. It was written in '96, before I knew him, but the four people mentioned are actual women. One was dead & three living when it was written – now only one is living ... 'Wessex Heights' will *always* wring my heart, for I know when it was written a little while after the publication of 'Jude', when he was so cruelly treated.

Hardy, at one time intending it to stand first in *SC*, withheld the poem from publication until 1914, no doubt because he suspected that its plaintive recollection of lost loves would wound Emma where, save for his agnosticism, he could most easily wound her. Several of the poem's references are probably oblique beyond scholarly straightening out, though if, as J. O. Bailey contends, ll. 5–6 refer to Emma (Bailey thinks the phrase 'not even' applies in apposition, past the dash, to 'Her ...': 'She is not even "Her who suffereth long and is kind"'), then clearly Hardy had another reason for not wanting Emma to read the poem. Bailey identifies Hardy's mother as 'the figure' in stanza five, Tryphena Sparks as all three ghosts in stanza six, and Mrs Henniker as the 'rare fair woman' in stanza seven (*Bailey*, pp. 275–9). *Gittings II*, pp. 123–7, offers different and more surmises.

'Ah, Are You Digging on My Grave?'

First published in the *Saturday Review*, 27 September 1913.

The Year's Awakening

First published in the *New Weekly*, 21 March 1914. A lovely poem, but one whose quality Hardy doubted in a letter to Frederic Harrison: 'Please don't look at the *New Weekly* – I mean my contribution to it. Scott-James came here one day, & I found that poor pair of stanzas in a drawer & could find nothing else, so I let him have them at his earnest request' (*Letters*, V, p. 21).

Under the Waterfall

Published 1914; but written in March 1913 during Hardy's stay in Cornwall. Hardy appears to have begun the poem in response to a passage in Emma Hardy's fragmentary memoir, *Some Recollections by Emma Hardy* (eds. Evelyn Hardy and Robert Gittings, 1961, p. 57), which he discovered among her effects:

We sketched and talked of books; often we walked down the beautiful [Vallency] Valley to Boscastle harbour where we had to jump over stones and climb over a low wall by rough steps, [or] get through by narrow pathways to come out on great wide spaces suddenly, with a sparkling little brook going the same way, into which we once lost a tiny picnic-tumbler, and there it is to this day no doubt between two small boulders.

Hardy quotes the passage in the *Life* (p. 71), revising it stylistically and adding this footnote: 'This incident was versified by Hardy afterwards, and entitled "Under the Waterfall".' His pencil-sketch of the episode, inscribed 'E. L. G. by T. H. Aug. 19, 1870', is reproduced in *Some Recollections*, between pages 56 and 57.

Poems of 1912–13

Emma Hardy died on 27 November 1912. During the next several months Hardy composed elegies in a sustained welling up of inspiration, writing 'more than he had ever written before in the same space of time' (*Life*, p. 361). 'The verses came,' he later remarked in a letter, 'it was quite natural. One looked back through the years and saw some pictures; a loss like that makes one's old brain vocal.' Hardy once called the elegies 'an expiation', both of his guilt over his years of inattention to Emma and of his remorse at the way their marriage had eroded the 'most childlike & trusting' (*Letters*, v, p. 64) woman he had fallen in love with in 1870.

On 6 March 1913 Hardy set out on a personal and poetic pilgrimage to St Juliot and the Cornish coast, where he and Emma had met and courted exactly forty-three years before, and to Plymouth, where Emma had lived with her family until she was nineteen. While he was on this trip Hardy wrote 'After a Journey', 'Beeny Cliff', 'At Castle Boterel', 'The Phantom Horsewoman' and 'St Launce's Revisited' (*Gittings II*, p. 209).

Because he was reluctant to expose his personal life so explicitly to readers who might only be put off or baffled by such exposure, Hardy hesitated before deciding to publish the sequence, writing to Edmund Gosse: 'I am . . . exercised on what to do with some poems. When I am dead & gone I shall be glad – if I can be anything – for them to have been printed, & yet I don't quite like to print them' (*Letters*, v, p. 35). No doubt it was Hardy's conviction that several of the poems were as good as any he had written that compelled him to overcome his reluctance; he was disappointed that the reviewers of *SC* all but ignored them (*Letters*, v, p. 70).

The epigraph is from the *Aeneid*, iv, 23: 'The traces of an old fire'. In *SC* the sequence consisted of just eighteen poems, but in *CP*, 1919, Hardy expanded the sequence by adding 'The Spell of the Rose', 'St Launce's Revisited' and 'Where the Picnic Was', three poems which had appeared in the 'Lyrics and Reveries' section of *SC*. In his essay 'Hardy's Virgilian Purples' (*Agenda*, 10, 1972, pp. 153–6) Donald Davie argues vigorously that the addition of the three poems violates Hardy's original argument. Most critics have agreed. Other valuable essays on the sequence include William Morgan, 'Form, Tradition and Consolation in Hardy's *Poems of 1912–13*' ('PMLA' 89, no. 3 [May 1974], pp. 496–505); J. Hillis Miller, *Thomas Hardy: Distance and Desire* (1970, *inter alia*); and Peter M. Sacks, 'Hardy: "A Singer Asleep" and *Poems of 1912–13*' (*The English Elegy*, 1985, pp. 227–59).

The Going

Published 1914. Hardy devotes two pages in the *Life* (pp. 359–60) to a summary of Emma's health during the six months prior to her death. With deliberate obscurity and some urgency Hardy writes that 'she was noticed to be weaker later on in the autumn, though not ill, and complained of her heart at times . . . She had not mentioned to her husband, or to anybody else so far as he could discover, that she had any anticipations of death before it occurred so suddenly.' Robert Gittings, for whom the 'omissions' Hardy reproaches himself with in the poem are too minor and commonplace to justify its depth of guilt and remorse, believes that Hardy was fully aware of the seriousness of Emma's condition (for months she suffered excruciating pain from impacted gallstones, which the death certificate cited as cause of death), but chose to ignore what he knew (*The Nature of Biography*, 1978, pp. 51–2):

When the enormity of this conduct was brought home to him by her death, he therefore had not mere minor, commonplace marital inconsiderations with which to reproach himself, but an indifference to a suffering human being and an actual physical neglect which amounted virtually to a crime. His use of the word 'expiation' was no exaggeration. The deeply felt remorse and self-horror of the poems becomes for the first time explicable in simple, physical terms alone, while one's whole view of Hardy as a man is also affected.

It may be, however, that Hardy's question in the first stanza of the poem and his exclamation in the last indicate at the worst only that despite Emma's months of affliction (during which, as Gittings knows, she continued to get out and to receive guests), perhaps precisely because of the chronic nature of the affliction, Hardy did not expect her 'swift' death.

Your Last Drive

Published 1914. In his notorious but in fact mostly laudatory review (*New Statesman*, 19 December 1914) of *SC*, Lytton Strachey objected to Hardy's 'ugly and cumbrous expressions, clumsy metres, and flat, prosaic turns of speech. To take a few random examples, in the second of the following lines cacophony is incarnate:

> Dear ghost, in the past did you ever find
> Me one whom consequence influenced much?'

Hardy revised the line.

The Walk

Published 1914. Three weeks after Emma's death Hardy wrote to Mrs Henniker (*Letters*, IV, p. 243):

In spite of the differences between us, which it would be affectation to deny, & certain painful delusions she suffered from at times, my life is intensely sad to me now without her. The saddest moments of all are when I go into the garden & to that long straight walk at the top that you know, where she used to walk every evening just before dusk, the cat trotting faithfully behind her; & at times when I almost expect to see her as usual coming in from the flower-beds with a little trowel in her hand.

The poem elicited a memorable remark from R. P. Blackmur: ' ... it is style reduced to anonymity, reduced to riches ...' ('The Shorter Poems of Thomas Hardy', *The Southern Review*, I, 1940, p. 47).

Rain on a Grave

Published 1914; written 31 January 1913 (*Gittings II*, p. 208).

'I Found Her Out There'

Published 1914. In *Some Recollections* (p. 50) Emma Hardy writes:

Scarcely any author and his wife could have had a much more romantic meeting with its unusual circumstances, in bringing them together from two different though neighbouring counties to this one at this very remote spot, with beautiful sea-coast, and the wild Atlantic ocean rolling in with its magnificent waves and spray, its white gulls and black choughs and grey puffins, its cliffs and rocks and gorgeous sunsettings sparkling redness in a track widening from the horizon to the shore.

Without Ceremony

Published 1914.

Lament

Published 1914.

The Haunter

Published 1914.

The Voice

Published 1914. Hardy saw into print two versions of l. 11 – 'You being ever consigned to existlessness' (*SC*) and then 'You being ever dissolved to existless-ness' (*CP*, 1919) – before settling (*CP*, 1923) on the phrasing printed here. I. A. Richards heard in the phrase 'in its listlessness' (l. 9) an allusion to the exchange between Nicodemus and Jesus in John 3:8–9: 'The wind bloweth where it listeth, and thou hearest the sound thereof, but canst not tell whence it cometh, and whither it goeth: so is every one that is born of the Spirit. Nicodemus answered and said unto him, How can these things be?' ('Some Notes on Hardy's Verse Forms', *Victorian Poetry*, 1/2, 1979, p. 6).

In the *Life* (p. 78) Hardy gives a more circumstantial description of the experience in stanza two. Arriving in Cornwall after several weeks in London, Hardy 'found the "young lady in brown" of the previous winter – at that time thickly muffled from the wind – to have become metamorphosed into a young lady in summer blue, which suited her fair complexion far better; and the visit was a most happy one.'

His Visitor

Published 1914. Emma Hardy was buried in Stinsford ('Mellstock'). In *SC* 'formal-fashioned' (l. 7) is 'brilliant budded'.

A Circular

Published 1914.

A Dream or No

Published 1914. In the *Life* (p. 104), commenting on what he saw as the novelist's need to live in society, Hardy writes of himself: 'Not that he was unsociable, but events and long habit had accustomed him to solitary living. So it was also with his wife, of whom he wrote later, in the poem entitled "A Dream or No".' Hardy then quotes ll. 10–12 of the poem, omitting the word 'There'.

This is the pivotal poem in the sequence. Hardy's mourning, not just over Emma's death, but over the disappearance years earlier of the 'maiden' he had married, moves him to wonder if she ever existed, out there in Cornwall or at Max Gate, and it is this question that propels him to make the pilgrimage that rediscovers her reality. In this sense I agree with Joseph Brodsky that 'the death of Emma Hardy releases, at least on paper, Emma Gifford into the world, allowing her to occupy the place, if not the tense, denied her in the present: she becomes a poem, the property of Art, the reality of language' ('The poet, the loved one and the Muse', *Times Literary Supplement*, 26 October–1 November 1990, p. 1160).

After a Journey

Published 1914. See F. R. Leavis, 'Reality and Sincerity: Notes in the Analysis of Poetry', *Scrutiny*, Winter 1952–3, pp. 87–98, for a justly famous discussion of the poem.

A Death-Day Recalled

Published 1914.

Beeny Cliff

Published 1914. Donald Davie, identifying *Aeneid*, VI, 640–41 – '*largior hic campos aether et lumine vestit/purpureo, solemque suum, sua sidera norunt*' – as the source of 'purples prinked the main' (l. 9), observes ('Hardy's Virgilian Purples', *Agenda*, 10, 1972, pp. 144–5):

Virgil's *purpureus* describes a light that is not any terrestrial light, however preternaturally radiant and keen; it is preternatural through and through, the light of an alternative cosmos, lit by another sun by day and other stars by night. And it is this light, no other, that Hardy, agnostic and scientific humanist, claimed to see from Beeny Cliff when 'purples prinked the main' . . . The status of Emma's *being*, now that she is dead – more than ever this metaphysical question seems to be the question that the poems ask . . .

Davie contends that the metaphysical answer to this question is that Emma has attained the status of a Dantesque spirit inhabiting for ever the natural sites she inhabited when Hardy first loved her.

At Castle Boterel

Published 1914.

Places

Published 1914. 'The term "beneaped" (l. 26) is used of a ship left aground by a neap tide; the reference is to Hardy himself, desolate after Emma's death' (*Bailey*, p. 305).

The Phantom Horsewoman

Published 1914.

The Spell of the Rose

Published 1914. 'Couched' (l. 39) refers to the surgical removal of a cataract.

St Launce's Revisited

Published 1914.

Where the Picnic Was

Published 1914.

The Newcomer's Wife

Published 1914. In *SC* this poem and the next six poems here appear in the section called 'Miscellaneous Poems'.

In the Servants' Quarters

Published 1914. The poem is based on John 18:15–27.

'Regret Not Me'

Published 1914.

The Recalcitrants

Published 1914. The poem's title was also one of Hardy's provisional titles for *Jude the Obscure*. The lover's mild exhortation to her beloved to retreat with her from the world's scrutiny to indifferent seclusion is something that Sue Bridehead might have said to Jude, particularly in Part V of the novel after they suffer the 'righteous judgement' (l. 12) of the people of Aldbrickham. Lois Deacon and Terry Coleman (*Deacon/Coleman*, pp. 207–10) speculate that the poem's lovers are Hardy and Tryphena Sparks, and that the motive behind the exhortation was Hardy's 'fear that his relationship with Tryphena had been incestuous', Hardy and Tryphena Sparks having been, Deacon and Coleman contend, not cousins but uncle and niece. For refutations of Deacon and Coleman's speculations, see D. J. Enright, 'Peeping at Tom' (*New Statesman*, 10 June 1966, pp. 846–7) and *Gittings I*, pp. 223–9. In his review of *Gittings I*, Philip Larkin remarked: 'The Deacon–Coleman solution may have been wildly and ludicrously wrong, but it *felt* true' (*New Statesman*, 18 April 1975, p. 515).

The Sacrilege

First published in the *Fortnightly Review*, 1 November 1911. *CP* prints 'sloe-back' (l. 29); I have followed James Gibson's correction to 'sloe-black' (*Thomas Hardy: The Complete Poems*, 1976, p. 400).

Exeunt Omnes

Published 1914. 'June 2, 1913' was Hardy's seventy-third birthday. In *SC* l. 15 reads 'So do I follow thither!'

In the Study

Published 1914. This poem and the next are numbers VIII and XV in 'Satires of Circumstance', the set of fifteen poems with which *SC* ends. As first published in the *Fortnightly Review* (April 1911) the set consisted of just twelve poems and did not include the two printed here.

In the *Life* (p. 367) Hardy comments on the odd and for him (as for later critics) dissatisfying relation between these poems and the rest of *SC*:

... he brought out another volume of verses entitled *Satires of Circumstance, Lyrics and Reveries* – the book being made up of the 'Satires in Fifteen Glimpses', published in 1911, and other poems of a very different kind with which the satires ill harmonized – the latter filling but fifteen pages in a volume of 230 pages. These were caustically humorous productions which had been issued with a light heart before the war. So much shadow, domestic and public, had passed over his head since he had written the satires that he was in no mood now to publish humour or irony, and hence he would readily have suppressed them if they had not already gained such currency from magazine publication that he could not do it. The 'Lyrics and Reveries', which filled the far greater part of the volume, contained some of the tenderest and least satirical verse that ever came from his pen.

The book's title may also have been a mistake, although, according to R. L. Purdy (*Thomas Hardy: A Bibliographical Study*, 1968, p. 172), the choice was not Hardy's but his publisher's.

In the Moonlight

Published 1914.

From *Moments of Vision and Miscellaneous Verses* (1917)

'We Sat at the Window'

Published 1917. Hardy and Emma were in Bournemouth in July 1875 (*Life*, p. 107).

Afternoon Service at Mellstock

Published 1917. As Hardy notes in the *Life* (p. 18), the poem recalls the years when as a boy of nine and ten he attended the Anglican services in Stinsford church. In 1926 Hardy made an effort to raise money on behalf of the church (*Letters*, VII, p. 9).

In a Museum

Published 1917.

At the Word 'Farewell'

First published in *SP*.

Heredity

Published 1917.

Near Lanivet, 1872

Published 1917; but the headnote appears 'in the manuscript, deleted' (*Bailey*, p. 349). Bailey also notes that Hardy 'identified the handpost of the poem on the endpapers of Hermann Lea's copy of *Thomas Hardy's Wessex* as "Handpost on the St Austell Road"' (*ibid.*, p. 350). Hardy's jotting reveals more than his scrupulous attention to fact and his more than occasional preference for those of his poems that adhere to real events. Apparently, Hardy regarded the experience at the handpost as one of the salient experiences of his and Emma's courtship. But scholars disagree on why he did so. Michael Millgate points to Hardy's anxiety over his recent rejection by Emma's father, who had called Hardy 'a low-born churl' to his face, as the explanation of Hardy's emphasis in the next-to-last stanza on the crucifixion that *he*, not Emma, might come to suffer (*Millgate*, pp. 142-3). Robert Gittings reads the poem in light of the lovers' dialogue in 'The Chosen', a poem whose setting at a 'Christ-cross stone' may also be the handpost on the St Austell Road, and in which the man recounts to the woman the charms of the five women he has already loved. Gittings concludes (*Gittings I*, pp. 162-4):

It may give some hint of the stress of the occasion in Cornwall, if Hardy had admitted, or been forced to admit to Emma, that there had been a number of girls in his affections before her ... However lightly he may have glossed this at the time, Emma's 'crucifixion' may be said to have come in her fifties, when his *Wessex Poems* produced publicly his poems to all these loves; even the assurance of her own friends could not prevent her from feeling exposed and humiliated. Quite literally, at that time, she mourned to a friend, 'alas ... The *thorn* is in my side still', actually using some sort of muddled crucifixion image of her own to express her wounded, martyred feelings.

Thom Gunn finds the poem mysterious in the manner of the Ballads, but appears to hear it as an expression of Hardy's realization that as for his life with Emma and hers with him his 'worst fears have been justified' (*Gunn*, p. 96).

Timing Her

Published 1917.

The Blinded Bird

Published 1917. The third stanza draws on 1 Corinthians 13.

The Faded Face

Published 1917. 'Weeted' (l. 12) is 'Listed' in *MV*.

Sitting on the Bridge

Published 1917.

The Oxen

First published in *The Times*, 24 December 1915; then in *SP*. In *The Times*, 'would weave' (l. 9) was 'believe'.

In his correspondence with Edmund Gosse in 1898, Hardy wondered 'if the custom you allude to, of the Cevenol cattle being brought to the church door on Xmas night, is of the same pedigree as the belief still held in remote parts hereabout, that the cattle kneel at a particular moment in the early hours of every Christmas morning – just at, or after, 12, I think?' (*Letters*, II, pp. 188-9). This anthropological curiosity gives way in the poem, written seventeen years later during the 'gloom' of the First World War, to Hardy's longing to reclaim, if only it were rationally possible, the blessings of those beliefs he himself once held.

An Anniversary

Published 1917.

Transformations

Published 1917. The poem gives what is perhaps Hardy's most moving response, at once naturalistic and emotionally Christian, to the elegiac question of what happens to the dead. Donald Hall's reading of the poem in *The Pleasures of Poetry* (1971, pp. 68–74) is superb.

The Mellstock edition (1920, vol. XXXVII) of Hardy's works has 'vainly' for 'often' in l. 11.

The Last Signal

Published 1917. Hardy first met William Barnes in 1856 when he worked as an architect's apprentice in an office next door to Barnes's school in Dorchester. They were friends for thirty years. If anyone may be said to have been Hardy's literary master, it was Barnes. On 11 November 1886 Hardy wrote to Coventry Patmore, 'Your criticism of Barnes's work was most instructive. I have lived too much within his atmosphere to see his productions in their due perspective, as you see them' (*Letters*, I, p. 157). Hardy wrote three prose pieces on Barnes: in 1879, a review of Barnes's *Poems of Rural Life in the Dorset Dialect*; in 1886, an obituary, 'The Rev. William Barnes, B.D.', for *The Athenaeum*; and in 1908, the preface to the *Select Poems of William Barnes*, which Hardy edited (see Appendix 1). For an excellent account of Barnes's literary influence on Hardy, see *Hynes*, pp. 23–33.

Great Things

Published 1917.

Overlooking the River Stour

Published 1917. In the *Life* (pp. 111–12) Hardy describes the life he and Emma shared during the nearly two years, from July 1876 to March 1878, that they rented a 'pretty cottage overlooking the Dorset Stour': 'It was their first house and, though small, probably that in which they spent their happiest days. Several poems commemorate their term there . . .' In June 1916, Hardy visited the house again for the first time since 1878, and 'it was possibly this visit which suggested the poems about Sturminster that were published in *Moments of Vision*' (*ibid.*, p. 373). For a description of the River Stour at Sturminster Newton, see *Bailey*, p. 382. *Millgate* reproduces a photograph of the 'cottage' between pp. 304 and 305.

Donald Davie, for whom Hardy is *the* late Victorian poet who possessed imagination enough to address the technological 'nature and life style' of the era, regards the poem as

all too shiningly, the work of a 'superb technician' who dismays us precisely by his *superbia*. The symmetries, stanza by stanza, are all but exact to begin with; once we know that the occasional inexactitude is no less engineered, 'engineered' seems more than ever the only word to use . . . there is an analogy with Victorian civil engineering, which topped off an iron bridge or a granite waterworks with Gothic finials, just as Hardy tops off his Victorian diction with an archaism like 'sheen' or 'alack'. Within its historically appropriate diction, the poem is 'a precision job'; that is to say, its virtuosity is of a kind impossible before conditions of advanced technology.

Davie goes on to say that Hardy 'is right to reproach himself' for his failure to perceive the importance 'of the human presence, Emma's, in the room behind him', and concludes that the poem gives us 'some sense of what it was like to be married to a Victorian engineer (whether in steel or in language)' (*Davie*, pp. 22–5). But Tom Paulin rightly points out that Davie 'doesn't appear to realize' that in the poem Hardy compares organic things to machines 'in order to stress the sterility of his positivism' (*Paulin*, pp. 170–71). In other words, Hardy's self-reproach precedes Davie's reproach of him. Still, in the last line, 'less', an example of Hardy's habit of trimming a word to make it fit the rhythm or rhyme (he trims the same word in the line 'The Less and Greater Bear', in 'Shut Out That Moon'), supports the first part of Davie's argument.

The Musical Box

Published 1917.

Old Furniture

Published 1917. Though weakened by weary self-approval in the final stanza, the poem expresses as well as any of Hardy's poems the household humanism that lies at the heart of his work. The *Life* (p. 116) states the gist of it memorably: 'An object or mark raised or made by man on a scene is worth ten times any such formed by unconscious Nature. Hence clouds, mists, and mountains are unimportant beside the wear on a threshold, or the print of a hand.'

The Last Performance

Published 1917; but written in December 1912 (*Gittings II*, p. 208). In the *Life* (p. 359) Hardy again describes how shortly before her death Emma 'played a long series of her favourite old tunes, saying at the end she would never play any more'.

The Interloper

Published 1917, but without the epigraph, which Hardy added after Vere Collins (*Talks with Thomas Hardy*, 1928, p. 25) told him he found the poem mysterious. Thom Gunn thinks that the poem is mystifying without the epigraph, but dully explicit with it (*Gunn*, pp. 86–7). Michael Millgate writes that 'Sir Clifford Allbutt, as a Commissioner in Lunacy, once gave it as his unofficial opinion that Emma was probably certifiable', and suggests that Hardy 'believed that the symptoms of Emma's condition . . . were visible, had he been able to recognize them, from the time of their first meeting' (*Millgate*, pp. 482–3).

Line 31 alludes to Daniel 3:24–5.

Logs on the Hearth

Published 1917, without the subtitle. In *MV* each stanza has five lines, with the refrain 'That time O!' appearing as the third line in each. The 'Sister' is Hardy's beloved Mary, who died on 24 November 1915 at the age of seventy-three.

The Sunshade

Published 1917.

The Five Students

Published 1917.

The Wind's Prophecy

Published 1917.

During Wind and Rain

Published 1917. In *MV* l. 14 reads 'See, the webbed white storm-birds wing across', and l. 28 has 'chiselled' for 'carved'.

Yvor Winters ('The Poetry of Louise Bogan', *New Republic*, 16 October 1929, p. 248) was the first critic to single out this poem as perhaps Hardy's greatest. Since he did so the ante has been very high: Tom Paulin has called it 'the best poem in *Moments of Vision* and one of the best poems of this century' (*Paulin*, p. 205); Randall Jarrell declared it 'one of the best poems anybody ever wrote' (*Randall Jarrell's Letters*, ed. Mary Jarrell, 1985, p. 240).

Before the discovery and publication of Emma Hardy's *Some Recollections* (1961) readers of the poem seemed to be in simple agreement that, however magnificent, the poem is just one of dozens that demonstrate Hardy's 'power to juxtapose a desolate present with an incompatible past' (Douglas Bush, *Thomas Hardy*, 1954, p. 150). It was assumed that the poem's images were impersonal, archetypal, with 'no distinction or force of their own' (*ibid.*, p. 148). But, as Robert Gittings observed (*Some Recollections*, 1961, pp. 67-8), Emma's memoir revealed that

The scene . . . is Plymouth, the family Emma Hardy's, and the details taken from the two chief houses in which they lived. It is likely that the dominant refrain was suggested by her own phrase , 'all has been changed with the oncoming years' . . .

What is perhaps most striking is that the whole idea of the poem and even its title *During Wind and Rain* derives from Emma Hardy's own feelings on leaving Plymouth. In *Some Recollections*, p. 37, she writes of being seen off at Plymouth station by young friends, who shared their family pleasures, in these words: 'The heavens poured down a steady torrent on our farewells, and never did so watery an omen portend such dullnesses, and sadnesses and sorrows as this did for us.' Whatever actual watery storm may have precipitated the poem, these words, in a page of the manuscript marked in Hardy's handwriting and so clearly read by him, provided the clue for the mood of the poem, with its description of his wife's happy but lost childhood and the dispersal by death of her family.

Some critics have objected to Gittings's conflation of the poem and its source. Paulin maintains that the memoir's 'details . . . are just so many rather fascinating facts, and it would be both terribly wrong and reductively Hobbesian to make Hardy's imagination wholly dependent on them, for, naturally, his imagination transformed them . . .' (*Paulin*, p. 208). Thom Gunn, while acknowledging that Hardy's 'thoughts about his wife's family' were the 'source' of the poem, offers the same conventional reminder: 'a work is not the same as its source' (*Gunn*, p. 90).

The poem needs to be read where Hardy placed it in *MV*, between 'The Wind's Prophecy' and 'He Prefers Her Earthly'. In the former, Hardy travels to the West Country to meet, as the wind announces, his true 'Love' [Emma], one whose 'tresses' are 'flashing fair'; in the latter, he says that, though Emma may now be part of the sunset's 'glory-show', he would prefer to go on remembering her as the 'fond and fragile creature' she was once. Like these two poems, 'During Wind and Rain' arises from Hardy's desire to restore Emma, if only on the page, to her youth, to the life she lived before not just their marriage but the change in circumstances that put her in a position ever to meet him, a desire he must have heard Emma herself expressing in her memoir (*Some Recollections*, 1961, p. 34):

When my dear Grandmamma died at Bedford Terrace in 1859 [1860?] we had to retrench on account of her income being divided, and it was decided to go to Cornwall. We left Plymouth in June of that year and it was for ever lost to me, for I have seldom visited it since; no county has ever been taken to my heart like that one ... its loveliness of place, its gentleness, and the generosity of the people are deeply impressed upon my memory ... Cornwall was very strange at first, after we had had to leave our very pleasant home. [And] Soon troubles began.

Her marriage and her final removal to Max Gate were the last stages in Emma's history of 'troubles' that began with the move to Cornwall. This is the emotional force, I think, behind the refrain, 'Ah, no; the years, the years'. The plangent denial is Emma's, spoken by Hardy for both of them.

He Prefers Her Earthly

Published 1917.

'Who's in the Next Room?'

Published 1917.

The Something That Saved Him

Published 1917; but written perhaps as early as 1869.

The Shadow on the Stone

Published 1917. Of the 'Druid stone', Hardy wrote (*Life*, pp. 233–4):

This was a large block they [the builders of Max Gate] discovered about three feet underground in the garden, and the labour of getting it from the hole where it had lain for perhaps two thousand years was a heavy one even for seven men with levers and other appliances – 'It was a primitive problem in mechanics, and the scene was such a one as may have occurred in building the Tower of Babel.' Round the stone, which had been lying flat, they had found a quantity of ashes and half charred bones.

For a photograph of Hardy standing admiringly beside the stone, see *Millgate*, between pp. 320 and 321.

'For Life I Had Never Cared Greatly'

Published 1917.

The Pity of It

First published in the *Fortnightly Review*, 1 April 1915; then in the *Dorset Year-book* for 1916–17; and then in a pamphlet that Hardy and his wife had printed. This and the poem that follows here appear in a section of seventeen 'Poems of War and Patriotism' in *MV*.

Hardy gave his view of the cause of the Great War in a letter to Mrs Henniker: 'I, too, like you, think the Germans happy & contented as a people: but the group of oligarchs & munition-makers whose interest is war, have stirred them up to their purposes – at least so it seems. I have expressed the thought in a sonnet . . .' (*Letters*, v, p. 86). When letters denouncing the poem were printed in the *Daily News*, he wrote again to Mrs Henniker: 'People are in strangely irritable moods I fancy. I said very harmlessly . . . that the Germans were a "kin folk, kin tongued" (which is indisputable) & letters attacking me appeared, denying it! The fact of their being our enemies does not alter their race' (*ibid.*, p. 215).

In Time of 'The Breaking of Nations'

First published in the *Saturday Review*, 29 January 1916; then in *SP*. Hardy composed the poem in 1915 from notes he had made at St Juliot on 18 August 1870 (*Millgate*, pp. 128, 502). He later pointed to this delay in composition as evidence of his 'faculty . . . for burying an emotion in my heart or brain for forty years, and exhuming it at the end of that time as fresh as when interred' (*Life*, p. 378).

For *MV* Hardy changed 'fade' to 'cloud' (l. 11). His reference in the footnote to Jeremiah 51:20 – 'Thou *art* my battle ax *and* weapons of war: for with thee will I break in pieces the nations, and with thee will I destroy kingdoms' – covers only the poem's title. Verses 21–3 are as apposite:

And with thee will I break in pieces the horse and his rider; and with thee will I break in pieces the chariot and his rider;

With thee also will I break in pieces man and woman; and with thee will I break in pieces old and young; and with thee will I break in pieces the young man and the maid;

I will also break in pieces with thee the shepherd and his flock; and with thee will I break in pieces the husbandman and his yoke of oxen; and with thee will I break in pieces captains and rulers.

The Coming of the End

Published 1917. This poem and the next make up the section called 'Finale' in *MV*. The poem draws on 1 Corinthians 15, which, Robert Gittings notes, was Hardy's 'second favourite passage' in the Bible, and one which as a young man he heard read as 'the second lesson at evening service on Tuesday in Easter Week, and which he marked at various times and at various dates when he heard it. It is also, of course, the chapter on resurrection, read at the service for the burial of the dead' (*Gittings I*, p. 50).

Afterwards

Published 1917. 'The simplest and most obvious thing that one can say about Hardy is that he had the best eye for natural detail in all British poetry' (Yvor Winters, *Forms of Discovery*, 1967, p. 189).

From *Late Lyrics and Earlier* (1922)

Weathers

First published in *Good Housekeeping* (London), May 1922. 'Bills his best' (l. 5) illustrates Hardy's habit of converting a substantive into a verb; see also, among dozens of instances, 'Or lip me the softest call' ('The Going') and 'The man foots in front of the horse' ('No Buyers'). Defending Hardy against the complaint that 'his diction is often quaint', Philip Larkin observed that 'often . . . the quaintness, if it is quaintness, is a kind of striving to be accurate. He might say, "I lipped her", when he means, "I kissed her", but after all, that brings in the question of lips and that is how kissing's done' ('The Poetry of Hardy', in *Required Writing*, 1982, p. 176).

Faintheart in a Railway Train

First published in the *London Mercury*, January 1920. Ezra Pound, an ardent admirer of Hardy's poetry, remarked, '*Carpe diem* never so coupled to an almost surprise that it, the day, should have been seized, and usually wasn't' (Appendix 1, *From Confucius to Cummings*, eds. Ezra Pound and Marcella Spann, 1964, p. 325).

The Garden Seat

Published 1922. Eugenio Montale's translation of this poem appears in *Agenda*, 10, 1972, p. 76.

'The Curtains Now Are Drawn'

Published 1922.

Going and Staying

First published in the *London Mercury*, November 1919, with the stanzas unnumbered and without stanza three.

A Wet August

Published 1922.

'A Man Was Drawing Near to Me'

Published 1922. The poem, in which Emma remembers herself as she was on the day (7 March 1870) that Hardy arrived at the rectory in St Juliot, draws on Emma's own meditation in *Some Recollections* (pp. 46-55).

The Strange House

Published 1922. 'The worst of taking a furnished house is that the articles in the rooms are saturated with the thoughts and glances of others' (*Life*, p. 254).

A Night in November

Published 1922.

'And There Was a Great Calm'

First published in the 'Armistice Day Section' of *The Times*, 11 November 1920; then in a pamphlet that Hardy and Florence Hardy had printed (1920). Hardy takes the title from Matthew 8:26: 'And he saith unto them, Why are ye fearful, O ye of little faith? Then he arose, and rebuked the winds and the sea; and there was a great calm.'

On the day the poem appeared in *The Times*, Hardy wrote to Harold Child: 'The Armistice supplement makes a very good show. I am afraid I must have been rather obscure, for the writer of the leading article on the subject seems to think I ask, why did the Allies fight? But the meaning is, of course, why did the War originate: why did those who started it, whoever they were, do so. – So far it looks as if they were the Germans, as we have all along supposed' (*Letters*, VI, p. 45). Before and then again several years after the war, Hardy called his view of history 'evolutionary meliorism' (see Appendix II, p. 200); but, as ll. 21–2 and the tender but ineffectual rejoinder of the final line indicate, the war temporarily quashed Hardy's faith in the notion.

'If It's Ever Spring Again'

Published 1922.

The Fallow Deer at the Lonely House

Published 1922.

At Lulworth Cove a Century Back

Published 1922.

Evelyn G. of Christminster

Published 1922. Evelyn Gifford was Emma Hardy's cousin. Hardy's journal entry for 6 September 1920 reads: 'Death of Evelyn Gifford, at Arlington House, Oxford. Dear Evelyn! whom I last parted from in apparently perfect health ... the poem "Evelyn G. of Christminster" was written on this occasion' (*Life*, p. 407).

Voices from Things Growing in a Churchyard

First published in the *London Mercury*, December 1921; then in a pamphlet that Hardy and Florence Hardy had printed (1922). Michael Millgate notes that the poem 'was written in 1921, stimulated in part by the experience, in January of that year, of reading through some of the old Stinsford parish registers ...' (*Millgate*, p. 540). Of the speakers in the poem, Hardy knew only the first, 'poor

Fanny Hurd', whose 'real name was Fanny Hurden, and Hardy remembered her as a delicate child who went to school with him. She died when she was about eighteen ...' (*Life*, pp. 413–14). 'The others mentioned in the poem', Hardy remarks, 'were known to him by name and repute' (*ibid.*, p. 414). Two died long before Hardy's birth, the last, 'old Squire Audeley Grey', at the beginning of the eighteenth century. See *Works*, II, pp. 514–15, and *Bailey*, pp. 462–4, for sketches of all five.

On the Way

Published 1922. For an account of the poem's debt to Shelley's *Epipsychidion*, see *Paulin*, pp. 138–41.

'She Did Not Turn'

Published 1922.

A Two-Years' Idyll

Published 1922. On 18 March 1878 Hardy noted (*Life*, p. 118): 'End of the Sturminster Newton idyll ...' The following is written in later: 'Our happiest time'. J. O. Bailey's contention (*Bailey*, p. 466) that it was perhaps Hardy's desire for 'greater success or fame' and Emma's 'for life in London' that led them to regard their happiness at Sturminster as 'Nought' is surely mistaken. If a specific motive informs the poem's lament – that after a time of real but unheeded happiness the Hardys' marriage declined into misery – it may be, as Robert Gittings has suggested, that the Hardys 'remained childless to the end' (*Gittings II*, p. 29).

By Henstridge Cross at the Year's End

As 'By Mellstock Cross at the Year's End', first published in the *Fortnightly Review*, 1 December 1919, without the headnote; then in 1922, with the last stanza heavily revised.

'If You Had Known'

Published 1922. Hardy must have composed the poem in March 1920, for it commemorates the first days he spent with Emma (March 1870). The title in manuscript was originally 'If I Had Known', and the poem spoken in the first person (James Gibson, *The Complete Poems of Thomas Hardy*, 1976, p. 965).

Fetching Her

Published 1922.

'Could I but Will'

Published 1922.

Without, Not Within Her

Published 1922.

Vagg Hollow

Published 1922. Hardy's entry in his journal for 20 April 1902 was perhaps the basis of the poem: 'Vagg Hollow, on the way to Load Bridge (Somerset) is a place where "things" used to be seen – usually taking the form of a wool-pack in the middle of the road. Teams and other horses always stopped on the brow of the hollow, and could only be made to go on by whipping. A waggoner once cut at the pack with his whip: it opened in two, and smoke and a hoofed figure rose out of it' (*Life*, p. 314).

First or Last

Published 1922.

The Marble Tablet

Published 1922. Emma was buried beside Hardy's family in Stinsford. In March 1913, after revisiting the church in St Juliot '. . . with which she had been so closely associated as organist before her marriage', Hardy arranged for the memorial tablet that he had designed to be placed in the church (*Life*, p. 361).

Last Words to a Dumb Friend

Published 1922. Like 'Could I but Will' and other poems Hardy wrote in old age, this poem on the death of one of Hardy's several beloved cats (Robert Gittings identifies her as 'Snowdove', *Gittings II*, p. 70) implicitly upbraids the Christian God for neglecting His creatures. Although the human 'Powers' have been no more able than God to prevent the cat's 'tragic end', they feel for it an enduring love that is divine.

The Sailor's Mother

First published in the *Anglo-Italian Review*, September 1918; then in 1922. The poem retells the end of 'To Please His Wife', a story Hardy first published in *Life's Little Ironies* (1894).

Intra Sepulchrum

Published 1922.

The Whitewashed Wall

First published in *Reveille*, November 1918; then in 1922. The magazine was 'devoted to the disabled sailors and soldiers' of the Great War (*Bailey*, p. 494). Hardy wrote to its editor, John Galsworthy, who had asked him to contribute a poem: 'Here are a few humble lines for *Reveille*, which may have at least the negative merit that nothing particular can be said against them. The fact is that I cannot do patriotic poems very well – seeing the other side too much' (*Letters*, v, p. 275).

In a London Flat

Published 1922.

Drawing Details in an Old Church

Published 1922.

An Ancient to Ancients

First published in *Century Magazine*, May 1922. See *Bailey*, pp. 489–99, for information on the names in this 'humorous commentary on Victorian culture'.

From *Human Shows, Far Phantasies, Songs and Trifles* (1925)

Waiting Both

First published in the *London Mercury*, November 1924. The poem arises from Job 14:14. In 1919, Hardy wrote to Handley Moule, then Bishop of Durham (*Life*, pp. 390–91):

You may agree with me in thinking it a curious coincidence that the evening before your letter arrived, & when it probably was just posted, we were reading a chapter in Job, & on coming to the verse: 'All the days of my appointed time will I wait, till my change come,' I interrupted & said: 'that was the text of the Vicar of Fordington [Moule's father] one Sunday evening about 1860.' And I can hear his voice repeating the text as the sermon went on – in the way they used to repeat it in those days – just as if it were but yesterday.

A Bird-Scene at a Rural Dwelling

First published in *Chambers's Journal*, November 1924. Samuel Hynes notes that the poem marked 'the sixtieth anniversary of Hardy's first publication, the prose sketch "How I Built Myself a House", which appeared, also in *Chambers's*, in 1865' (*Works*, III, p. 311).

The Later Autumn

First published in the *Saturday Review*, 28 October 1922. Robert Gittings (*Gittings I*, pp. 49–50) sees the poem as evidence of Hardy's debt to the 'complicated metrical devices' of John Keble's *The Christian Year* (1827).

In l. 9, '"Toadsmeat" seems to be toads-cheese, a poisonous fungus' (*Bailey*, p. 507).

An East-End Curate

First published in the *London Mercury*, November 1924.

The Month's Calendar

Published 1925. The poem is addressed to Mrs Henniker, whom Hardy met in May 1893. By that July, 'Hardy had already begun to realize that Mrs Henniker's views upon morality in general and marriage in particular were likely to prove too rigidly conventional to allow of any relationship that went beyond the strictly "platonic"' (*Millgate*, p. 338). The date of composition is uncertain; Hardy may well have written it from notes following Mrs Henniker's death in April 1923.

When Dead

Published 1925.

Night-Time in Mid-Fall

Published 1925.

A Sheep Fair

Published 1925.

Snow in the Suburbs

Published 1925. An 'anthology' poem of the kind that, according to Florence Hardy, Hardy said a month before his death it had been his 'only ambition' to write and see included 'in a good anthology like the Golden Treasury' (*Life*, p. 444).

Samuel Hynes (*Works*, III, p. 313) notes that Hardy's alternative title was 'Snow at Upper Tooting'; the Hardys lived in Upper Tooting from 1878 to 1881. But the poem's matter-of-fact cadence and plain phrasing ('The palings are glued together like a wall') are characteristic of Hardy's final style. Donald Davie goes so far as to call the poem 'an Imagist equation' (*Davie*, p. 47).

Ice on the Highway

Published 1925.

No Buyers

Published 1925.

The Weary Walker

First published in *Bermondsey Book*, December 1925.

Nobody Comes

Published 1925. The poem records Hardy's waiting at the front of Max Gate for Florence Hardy to return home from hospital after having undergone an operation on her neck (*Millgate*, pp. 554–5). That 'nobody comes' to relieve isolation and sorrow is a recurrent motif in Hardy's work. A well-known example is the passage in chapter IV, First Part, of *Jude the Obscure* (1895): 'Somebody might have come along that way who would have asked him his trouble, and might have cheered him ... But nobody did come, because nobody does ...'

Last Look round St Martin's Fair

Published 1925.

When Oats Were Reaped

Published 1925

The Harbour Bridge

Published 1925. The setting is 'Weymouth, where a bridge crosses the River Wey at a point where the Wey turns eastward toward the sea' (*Bailey*, p. 539).

'Not Only I'

Published 1925. The speaker may be Emma, the faith in redemption hers.

Horses Aboard

Published 1925. In August 1899, Hardy bicycled to Southampton to watch the troops depart for South Africa; but the poem's idiom points to the 1920s as the likely time of composition.

The Missed Train

First published in *The Owl*, Winter 1923; then in L. A. G. Strong, ed., *Best Poems of 1924*, Boston, 1924 (*Works*, III, p. 106). John Crowe Ransom's praise is merited. The last two stanzas, he remarked, are 'beautiful and final. We feel that this is the only way, in just these verses word for word as they stand, for the old poet to conclude his very late poem' (*Ransom*, p. 87).

Cynic's Epitaph

First published in the *London Mercury*, September 1925.

The Sundial on a Wet Day

Published 1925.

Shortening Days at the Homestead

Published 1925. 'This autumn [1873] Hardy assisted at his father's cider-making – a proceeding he had always enjoyed from childhood – the apples being from huge old trees that have now long perished. It was the last time he ever took part in a work whose sweet smells and oozings in the crisp autumn air can never be forgotten by those who have had a hand in it' (*Life*, p. 96).

Days to Recollect

Published 1925. 'Saint Alban's Head' (l. 3) stands near Swanage, where Hardy and Emma spent the summer in 1875 (*Millgate*, pp. 177–9).

The High-School Lawn

Published 1925.

'Nothing Matters Much'

Published 1925. The poem's subject is Judge Benjamin Fossett Lock (*Letters*, VI, p. 364). 'The Flamborough' is a promontory near Bridlington in Yorkshire, where Judge Lock died on 11 August 1922 (*Bailey*, pp. 566–7).

'Why Do I?'

Published 1925.

From *Winter Words in Various Moods and Metres* (1928)

'I Am the One'

Published 1928.

The Mound

Published 1928. Lois Deacon and Terry Coleman (*Deacon/Coleman*, pp. 113–14) speculate that 'Tryphena and Hardy are the persons of the poem', and that the scene is the eweleaze near Puddleton. But Robert Gittings asserts that 'the girl . . . is surely the one on whom Sue in *Jude* is based, for the poem is parallel to Sue's confession, in Jude's lodging, of her past life' (*Gittings II*, p. 277). These might be the same conclusion.

Evening Shadows

First published in the *Daily Telegraph*, 7 May 1928.

Throwing a Tree

First published as 'Felling a Tree' in *Commerce*, Winter 1928, with a translation by Paul Valéry. The poem, which, contrary to the note in *Commerce* and the rumour it gave rise to, was not Hardy's last, is substantially a reworking of William Barnes's 'Vellen o' the tree' (1879).

Lying Awake

First published in the *Saturday Review*, 3 December 1927. 'It's as though the star is deputizing for God in an agnostic version of a Berkeleyan system . . . The last line is hushed and miraculous, a positivist's idea of the resurrection where the dead come "creeping out" as the growing light, like a focusing eye, makes their names and memorials legible. This is the real resurrection' (*Paulin*, pp. 119–20).

He Never Expected Much

First published in the *Daily Telegraph*, 19 March 1928.

Standing by the Mantelpiece

Published 1928. The initials of the headnote stand for Horace Mosley Moule, the speaker of the poem, who killed himself in rooms at Cambridge on 21 September 1873. Moule was Hardy's first close friend, and his learning and literary opinions, expressed in conversations, letters and later in reviews of Hardy's books, were immensely valuable to the young writer.

The poem's Shakespearian phrasing – 'To-night. To me twice night, that should have been/The radiance of the midmost tick of noon' – seems to me less an attempt to dramatize the rhetoric of Horace Moule than a sign of Hardy's early saturation in the sonnets and plays. That Hardy wrote the poem soon after Moule's death seems likely.

Christmas: 1924

First published as 'Peace upon Earth' in the *Daily Telegraph*, 18 June 1928. On 25 February 1900, Hardy wrote to Mrs Henniker: 'We the civilized world have given Christianity a fair trial for nearly 2000 years, & it has not yet taught countries the rudimentary virtue of keeping peace: so why not throw it over, & try, say, Buddhism?' (*Letters*, II, p. 248).

'We Are Getting to the End'

First published in the *Daily Telegraph*, 28 May 1928.

He Resolves to Say No More

First published in the *Daily Telegraph*, 18 September 1928; but written in 1927 (*Bailey*, p. 627). John Berryman marvelled that this 'great lyric . . . was published posthumously in what would have been [Hardy's] eighty-eighth year' ('Hardy and His Thrush', in *The Freedom of the Poet*, 1976, p. 244), alluded to it in a line ('Tiny Hardy, toward the end, refused to say anything') in 'Dream Song 53' (*The Dream Songs*, 1969, p. 60), and modelled his late poem 'He Resigns' on it (*Delusions, etc.*, 1972, p. 40) – one sign of how Hardy's poems abide.

In l. 18, 'By truth made free', Hardy is remembering John 8:32: 'And ye shall know the truth, and the truth shall make you free.'

Appendix 1

Published as preface to Hardy's edition of the *Select Poems of William Barnes*, Clarendon Press, 1908.

Appendix 2

Published 1922.

Index of Titles

Index of First Lines